OPEN YOUR OWN
BED & BREAKFAST

Barbara Notarius
Gail Sforza Brewer

JOHN WILEY & SONS, INC.

New York · Chichester · Brisbane · Toronto · Singapore

Publisher: Stephen Kippur
Editor: Katherine S. Bolster
Managing Editor: Ruth Greif
Editing, Design, and Production: G&H/SOHO, Ltd.

Library of Congress Cataloging-in-Publication Data

Notarius, Barbara.
    Open your own bed and breakfast.

    Includes index.
    1. Bed and breakfast accommodations.   2. Hotel management.   I. Brewer, Gail Sforza.   II. Title.
TX911.2.N68   1987   647'.94'068   87-2189
ISBN 0-471-84856-5

Printed in the United States of America

87 88 10 9 8 7 6 5 4 3 2 1

Acknowledgments

Thanks for assistance and support for this book project go to:

- Doris Tomer, my partner, who believed in me and this business from the beginning and who has given untold hours of unpaid service to Bed & Breakfast, U.S.A.

- My husband, George Klein, for hours of unpaid editing and years of listening to me talk about nothing else than Bed and Breakfast.

- Pat Wilson and Sarah Sonke of the American Bed and Breakfast Association, a clearinghouse for B&B information.

- Betty Rundback, author of one of the first B&B guides, who testified at my zoning trial and helped make it possible to establish a legal precedent for Bed and Breakfast in residential neighborhoods.

- Steve Apesos, publicist for the "I Love NY" campaign.

- Connie Crawford, CPA, for information about the tax consequences of operating a Bed and Breakfast in your home.

- Cheryl Woods and Joseph Schilling of the New York State Department of Commerce.

- Susan Kizis, Deloria Chapin, and Honesty Buczek, regional representatives of Bed & Breakfast, U.S.A., Ltd., who help with home visits.

- Kate Peterson of Bed & Breakfast Rocky Mountains, Susan and Richard Kreibech of American Family Inn Bed & Breakfast, Susan Morris and Helen Heath of Southern Comfort Bed & Breakfast, Aster Mould of Bed & Breakfast New Jersey, Ruth Young of Mi Casa Su Casa, and all the other members of Bed & Breakfast Reservation Services Worldwide without whom our trade association would not be possible.

- Gary Craig, who introduced me to John Wiley & Sons Publishers.

- Betsy Perry, Susan Geis, and Katherine S. Bolster, our editors.

- Christine Webb, my nanny, whose good spirits and dedication has kept my home and family going when my attention was unavoidably elsewhere.

- All our hosts, who have taught me as much as I have taught them and without whom Bed and Breakfast could not exist.

Contents

Introduction: America Is Waking Up to Bed and Breakfast

Just seven years ago in the United States, one could find private-home Bed and Breakfast accommodations in only fifteen locations, primarily in California, with each host functioning as a sole entrepreneur. Today, over 20,000 families open their homes to paying guests, and most are linked coast to coast through a trade association of professional reservation services. Newsletters describing advances in the industry abound. Directories of establishments are published regularly. Major corporations include B&B travel memberships as executive perks and sales incentives. Indeed, the term *Bed and Breakfast* has become so popular that even national hotel chains claim to offer the service.

There has never been a better time to become part of the Bed and Breakfast movement. This book is dedicated to helping you open a B&B in your home—be it a single room in your apartment, a room that is available when your child is away at college, or a multibedroom country mansion you can't wait to restore and fill constantly with guests. This book will assist you in finding out what is unique about your area, your home, and yourself, for it is the personal approach to gracious hospitality that distinguishes B&B hosting from all other types of travel services.

This book is an outgrowth of seminars for prospective hosts that I have given as president of Bed & Breakfast U.S.A., Ltd. The seminars presented the basics of starting a B&B. Questions from audience members were encouraged. Some of the most common questions and their answers are included at the end of each chapter.

In this book, I go beyond the introductory seminars and provide very detailed business management information culled from hundreds of owners and the reservation services that I work with regularly. All this is offered in the hope that it will increase the joy and ease with which you manage your Bed and Breakfast. For most hosts, it is the pleasure that comes from adding new people to their lives that keeps them involved, not the intricacies of the latest Internal Revenue Service ruling on the tax consequences of home-based businesses. However, I will cover that, as well.

There have long been country inns, and many of the people attending my seminars think that they will learn how to run a country inn. But as you will see, a private-home B&B is not a country inn on a smaller scale; it is first and foremost a private home. It is a type of accommodation that is new to America, and its development has been very different from that of its precursors in Europe.

What makes me an expert on private-home Bed and Breakfast? Perhaps a brief description of how I became involved seven years ago will provide an answer.

OUR DREAM HOUSE

In 1981, when my husband and I bought our house, we were not looking for a 5,000-square-foot abode, but that's exactly what we fell in love with. My mother and most of Croton-on-Hudson, New York, looked at the house and saw a white elephant that had been on the market for a year and a half. All they could see was that the house needed massive cosmetic repair, and they were scared off by it. What my husband, George, and I saw was its potential to be the home of our dreams. I never thought we would be able to afford a house with a river view, an in-ground pool, and space for our family to grow and to enjoy our many hobbies.

What we failed to understand was that although we could definitely afford the mortgage, the maintenance costs of such a large house would become our undoing. We had lived in a normal four-bedroom colonial home in lower Westchester, New York, before coming to Croton. The movers laughed as they delivered our furniture. The contents of the entire first floor of our old house barely filled up the thirty-five-foot sun porch of our new one. And our new living room, dining room, and downstairs office and study were pitifully empty.

The first year, I took a part-time job as a psychologist a few hours a week and spent my entire salary on wallpaper, paint, and filling up the many empty rooms with treasures acquired at garage sales, estate sales, and auctions. All my free time (when my little daughter was napping) was spent atop a ladder, scraping off years of accumulated wallpaper, sealing cracks, painting ceilings, and putting up new wallpaper. The house began to look better.

After the first winter, my husband sat down with me to talk about the cost of making our dream house a reality. Our heating bill the first winter was over $5,000 for 4,300 gallons of fuel oil; and even with oil heat, our electric bill was more than $200 a month. Our property taxes had gone from $4,800 to $6,200 just because the house had changed hands and taxes were based on the new selling price. Every new project seemed to cost twice as much as we expected and took three times as long to complete. For example, when we uncovered the pool, we found ten broken coping stones (the cement blocks that rim the pool). Each one had to be cut separately to a paper pattern by hand by a professional stonecutter—a major project with a price to match.

Although our grand plan had been for me to be an at-home mom until our daughter, Cydney, reached school age, it became quite apparent that this scenario was only a dream. It began to look as though I would have to go back to a full-time job, or we would have to move into a smaller, more affordable home. After all the work I had done on the house, selling it was unthinkable. When I explored the idea of resuming my job in New York City, I realized that although on paper I earned $25,000, after paying taxes ($12,500), a baby-sitter ($7,000), transportation ($2,000), and maintaining a professional wardrobe ($2,000), what I would be earning for being gone from my home and child all day would be under $2,000. This was obviously not the solution. I knew I couldn't start a home-based business and expect to earn $25,000, but could I beat $2,000 after taxes? I bet that I could. Having a home-based business that would allow us to write off some of our outrageous maintenance costs looked better and better. Our assets—the spaciousness of the house, many unused bedrooms, our enjoyment of entertaining and offering gracious hospitality—were ripe with possibility.

OUR FIRST GUEST

Bill, our very first guest, came to us from Brisbane, Australia after reading about our service in the newspaper. He was sixty-seven years old and had traveled around the world twice before. On this trip, he had crossed Russia via the Trans-Siberian Railway and visited for a few weeks with his daughter in England. He wanted to break up the twenty-four-hour plane ride home. He decided to stay with us for a week of rest and relaxation and perhaps a little sightseeing in New York City. The day before he arrived, my husband was very worried that Bill would expect us to change our life during his visit. I pooh-poohed this, saying that non-Americans were much more familiar with the B&B concept and would not expect anything of the sort. Of course, secretly I was worried, too—needlessly, it turned out. Bill's stay with us was so enjoyable that the day before he left, George took the day off to spend more time with him. He was a thoroughly delightful guest, full of yarns and humorous stories about a land halfway around the world.

Bill wanted to visit New York City for one or two days, but only if he could see some interesting things that most tourists don't get around to. We put together a list of special places and he had a ball. What he was really interested in was sampling a slice of American life. He asked if he could tag along with me to the local supermarket, nursery school, and town meeting. These trips to places where I normally go without paying attention took on a new interest. Looking through Bill's eyes at what I took for granted made me appreciate my town, my life, and being an American.

The day Bill and I went to the supermarket for groceries, he was as overjoyed as a small child at a toy store. While standing at the deli counter, he told me that in Russia, he had been able to shop at an Intourist store (where the average Russian is not permitted) and there was told that the Russians have the best smoked salmon in the world. But what was being sold at our deli counter, available to anyone who wanted it, was every bit as good. At the poultry counter, he stared at the variety of turkey parts and remarked, "In Brisbane, we don't have to kill the bird ourselves anymore, but we still have to buy a whole bird. Consequently, most single folks only eat turkey in restaurants." I actually felt lucky coming out of the market that day.

In fact, by the time Bill left for home, I felt that Croton had to be one of the best places in the world to live. One of our most enjoyable afternoons together was after a snowfall. Along with my then three-year-old daughter, Bill went sledding down my neighbor's hill. It was the first time he had ever played in snow.

One evening, we attended a town zoning meeting because our neighbor down the street wanted his next-door neighbor to remove a rotting boat that was blocking his river view. Bill was amazed as various people got up to speak, and he celebrated our friend's victory with us afterward. Over a brandy, Bill remarked that in Australia there is no such forum for neighborhood disputes. "In all likelihood, the boat would have 'caught fire' one night, and that would have been that!"

During Bill's visit I called the local newspaper and they sent a reporter out to interview him. When the story appeared, I began receiving more and more calls from people asking how to get into the B&B business. The media coverage from our first guest had a snowball effect.

Bill's visit was an auspicious beginning, and both his and our lives were enriched by the experience. The first year, we earned $1,500. Six years later, we earned $15,000. And we are living a more enjoyable and unpressured life than many couples trying to maintain two full-time jobs and raise their families after hours.

BED & BREAKFAST U.S.A., LTD.

In the beginning, I had hoped that other host homes would join me so that we could share the cost of advertising and the work of answering phones and inquiries and doing promotion.

After the publicity surrounding Bill's visit, a number of people called me, interested in opening their homes but not in the myriad behind-the-scenes tasks needed to promote this new type of travel accommodation. They said they would prefer to pay a commission to an outside service to screen their guests, represent their Bed and Breakfast to the public, collect the money, and leave them free to enjoy their guests. That was how Bed & Breakfast U.S.A., Ltd., a reservation service, was born. It began in a spare room of my house and now is located in a storefront with many phone lines and with a staff to answer them, inspect and represent our host homes, and coordinate promotion for our network. We have had local as well as national coverage on radio and television and in magazines and newspapers. *Bed and Breakfast* has become a household term.

Recently, someone told me that she saw me as a pioneer of the eighties. This was the nicest thing anyone has ever said about me. But I don't think I'm alone in looking for ways to personalize more of my life. Leo Buscaglia, a professor and best-selling author of books about contemporary relationships, commented recently that the reason so many people have responded to his work is that they want to be treated as individuals. People want to be appreciated for themselves. I believe that the growing national interest in traveling in a less anonymous fashion, really coming to know your guests or hosts and sharing some of your life in the process is a part of this trend. Most of the people I meet who become hosts share these sentiments.

BED & BREAKFAST RESERVATION
SERVICES WORLDWIDE

Bed and Breakfast has so far been a grass-roots movement. Reservation services have helped people open their homes to guests, and there are currently more than 200 such services around the world. In 1985, Bed & Breakfast Reservation Services Worldwide, a nonprofit trade association, was formed to help its members work together to unify standards and promote private-home accommodations through education, advertising, and public-service announcements. In a few short years, it has been instrumental in opening up communication among reservation services, making Bed and Breakfast more easily available to travelers and travel agents, and educating both hosts and guests. If you live in an area where there is no reservation service and you are looking for a full-time job commitment, consider starting one. The financial rewards are not easily won, but the reward of helping hosts open their homes and offering a very special personal service to travelers is very great.

BECOME PART OF THE INDUSTRY NOW

I have served two years as president of Bed & Breakfast Reservation Services Worldwide and have seen the industry mature considerably. In 1985, the U.S. government estimated that less than one-tenth of one percent of the American public had ever stayed at a B&B but that a growing interest promises tremendous expansion. There is room in the industry for all who are sincere and capable.

1

Bed and Breakfast Defined: Basic Principles

B ed and Breakfast is a grass-roots movement that is beginning to take off across our country, gaining acceptance in many different kinds of communities and providing accommodations for an ever-increasing number of people who, for one reason or another, don't want or need to stay in the more traditional hotels and motels that dot the countryside. But what is Bed and Breakfast? Where did it come from? How will you know if Bed and Breakfast is for you?

INTERNATIONAL ORIGINS

Bed and Breakfast is a generic term for accommodations offered in private homes rather than commercial facilities such as hotels or motels. It began in Britain after World War II, when American soldiers were waiting for troop carriers to ship them back home. Many waited weeks for their turn to come and chose to use their extended leave to see a little of the country they had just helped. The courageous women who had gone to work in the airplane factories now were called upon to open their homes to these young men because there was far too little hotel space left standing to go around. The soldiers were charmed by these women, who shared with them stories about their locale, steered them to out-of-the-way restaurants and places of interest, and often called on friends or relatives in other parts of England to open their homes to these guests.

The women, in turn, enjoyed befriending these appreciative young men, and the few dollars that they were paid to offer a pleasant guest room and hearty morning meal were a way to buy luxuries long unavailable during wartime. They repaired and spruced up their homes, and many continued to offer B&B long after the soldiers had gone home and were replaced by American tourists. The tourists, who had been unable to travel during the war, flocked to England in large numbers.

Because B&B accommodations were initially made available at the request of the government, regulations were initiated. Once a B&B host was approved, a little sign went up outside the home so that travelers could easily find a place to stay. Not all hosts wished to have strangers ring the bell without warning, however, and many of the finer places became affiliated with booking agencies that matched up the appropriate guests and hosts and otherwise protected the hosts' privacy.

Even castles are sometimes available through such agencies—taking in B&B guests helps the owners to pay their taxes. In Great Britain today, as many as 40 percent of all overnight stays are spent in Bed and Breakfasts. Although literally a cottage industry, this is no small business.

WHY NOT AMERICAN B&B?

Popular plays in London are usually seen on Broadway within two years, and anything Princess Diana wears can be bought at major department stores practically the next day. But the Bed and Breakfast concept took forty years to become popular in America. It spread rapidly as *pensiones* in Italy, *zimmers frei* in Germany, and under many other names throughout Europe, but not in the United States. Many people ask, "Why?" The answer, I believe, lies in the system of supply and demand. In America, there used to be tourist homes in every village, often big old houses where the elderly owner took in boarders or roomers and also let rooms by the night to travelers passing through.

As our modern road system took shape, motor hotels or motels sprang up close to highway exits. Motorists could pull off when they became tired, knowing that they would find a clean, comfortable room at a reasonable price. Over time, the tourist homes deteriorated because fewer patrons drove through on local roads and the owners of tourist homes could no longer afford to keep up their places. The small mom-and-pop motels charged low rates and used the profits to support Mom and Pop rather than reinvest in the maintenance of their structures.

Motel chains sprang up. They promised no surprises, and that's what they gave you. At first, this was good. The American public liked the idea of uniform standards and patronized these motels in huge numbers. By the time most Americans can drive, they can close their eyes and describe the average chain motel, even down to the color of the bedspreads. The chains set up central booking agencies with toll-free 800 telephone numbers and did everything possible to attract the consumer. They were successful, but the ever rising hotel/motel costs began to turn some patrons away.

FIGHTING THE PLASTIFICATION OF AMERICA

In the late sixties, many American young people were tremendously dissatisfied with the way our culture was heading. As a reaction to being overprocessed, turned out by machine, and identified by numbers instead of being seen as individuals, people turned to organic foods, homemade meals, and handicrafts and away from synthetic materials, artificial coloring, and plastic. In the seventies and eighties, as the hippies became the yuppies and the average age of Americans rose, a demand developed for rediscovering the enriching travel that our grandparents enjoyed, travel that allowed you to get to know the people in other parts of our country, not just see the monuments. People who were struggling to restore historic houses yearned to really talk with others who had fought and won many of the same battles against years of past neglect. Those who live most of the year in a high-rise apartment building want to experience life on a farm or a yacht or in an old country house in the mountains; suburban families want to live for a few days in an apartment in a fast-paced city. By the early eighties, these factors combined with the dramatic jump in hotel prices to create the demand for Bed and Breakfast.

THE COUNTRY INN FANTASY

Country inns have long appealed to the traveler for their old-fashioned hospitality. Think "country inn," and what comes to mind is a sprawling older home in New England set back on a tranquil country lane. Ask any group of six people and you are likely to find that five will admit to fantasies of giving up their present way of life to run a country inn.

But fantasies are not reality. Few people actually relocate to live their idyllic dreams. To begin with, most people are unable to make such a drastic change in life-style. Moreover, a country inn is a serious commercial business. Success depends on good organization, substantial capital, publicity, promotion, advertising, and the ability to manage a staff, maintain buildings, and run a restaurant. There is considerable turnover in the country inn business. All too soon it can become apparent to an enthusiastic beginner that keeping the occupancy rate high and the guests and the staff happy leaves little time for personal pursuits. This is certainly not consistent with the fantasy of living a relaxing, and simpler life in the country.

THE COMMERCIAL INN

A commercial inn is a place that is open to the public, has a sign outside, may be privately or corporately owned, and usually has more than ten rooms, sometimes more than twenty. It is in an area that is either unzoned or commercially zoned and is usually required to be licensed by the state. A commercial inn must have approval and regular inspection by the health department, and is subject to all aspects of its state's fire and safety regulations and restaurant code. It usually has a restaurant that may be open for dinner and lunch as well as breakfast and that takes reservations from people who are not staying at the inn as well as from guests. An inn has a large staff, cleans its rooms and changes its linens on a daily basis, is open day and night to receive guests, and commits large amounts of time and money to promotion and advertising. In order to increase business, many inns also cater parties and weddings and are constantly on the lookout for other ways to keep their occupancy rate as high as possible.

PRIVATE-HOME BED AND BREAKFAST

Private-home Bed and Breakfasts are very different from commercial inns. Generally, they are located in residentially zoned areas, offer from one to five rooms, and have no sign outside. Usually, they belong to a reservation service through which they find most of their guests. They leave promotion and advertising to their reservation service, along with the screening of the guests and the collecting of deposits. As a rule, there is no staff to manage other than an occasional gardener, house-

13

keeper, or serviceman. The hosts have very different expectations and much less stress related to carrying on the business. They meet people from many cultures, earn extra income, and enjoy the tax advantages of using their homes for a business, but they do it at their own convenience. They take guests when they want, and although they enjoy the extra income, they don't expect to support themselves from it.

A private-home B&B is primarily a private home. It is a home where some business is done, not a place of business where people live. This may sound like a mere semantic distinction, but think for a moment of the implications. In a private home, the host and hostess are using their assets (extra bedrooms and genial personalities) to meet interesting people and earn some extra money. They can decide which types of guests they will enjoy being around and which they won't. If smokers or toddlers drive a host to distraction, he or she can restrict guests to nonsmokers or children over six. Naturally, such restrictions reduce the pool from which guests come and lower potential volume. But hosts who do not rely on B&B for a living can afford to do this. A commercial inn, which needs a certain occupancy rate to stay alive, cannot afford to be so choosy.

My classic response to those who want to know the difference between a private-home B&B and an inn is that it is similar to the difference between being a gourmet cook and a chef.

Staff and Overhead

In a commercial inn, the occupancy rate is crucial because a certain amount of business is necessary to show a profit. Overhead is considerable, and there are few ways to lower it in proportion to the decrease in business during seasonally slow periods. Staff laid off may not be available when they are needed again. Training new staff is costly, and most businesses strive to keep turnover as low as possible.

14

In a private home, little to no staff is necessary. Overhead costs for the family to reside there are raised only slightly by having extra guests. Yet a portion of those costs will be legitimate business expenses.

Guests' Expectations

In many respects, the difference in service between a B&B and a commercial facility is reflected in the rates charged. If you start charging luxury rates, guests will expect luxury service, too.

In a commercial inn, guests pay luxury prices and expect to be pampered, with telephones and televisions in their rooms and a maid waiting each morning to clean and to make up the bed. No matter when guests arrive, someone is expected to be waiting to greet them. In a private home, guests realize that host families have full and interesting lives outside of the home and that it is necessary to call in advance to arrange a mutually convenient arrival time. If they fail to do this, they may arrive to find a note on the door letting them know that the family is attending a child's soccer game and will return in a few hours.

Guests, too, behave differently toward the staff at a commercial inn and the hosts of a Bed and Breakfast. The less commercial the place, the more the hosts will be treated as new friends. Many times, private-home guests help to clear the breakfast table, share interesting recipes, and send thank-you notes or even presents. I know hosts who have received theater tickets from happy guests who couldn't use their subscription seats, potholders appliquéd with the host's name, and a variety of other creative thank-yous for warmth and hospitality.

Time Commitments

People who run a country inn or hotel know that theirs is a full-time job. Often, it seems like time and a half. B&B hosts commit only as much time to their business as they want to. Some B&B's are only open during a particular season, on weekends, or for a certain number of days each week or month. Guests don't usually come to sit around the house. They arrive with a list of places they want to see, usually too numerous to cram into the limited time they have. Others are visiting family or hospitalized friends or relatives, attending weddings, or house hunting. Once breakfast is over, guests disappear and may not be seen again until they come back to change for the evening. A few moments of consultation about making dinner reservations and plotting the route to the restaurant and they are off again.

Guests receive a key to the home and come and go at will. No one has to stay around twenty-four hours a day to baby-sit for the house. All guests come by advance reservation, and hosts have the opportunity to make sure that the larder is stocked for the expected arrivals and that the home and guest rooms are sparkling and ready for company. This leaves the hosts free to enjoy the other aspects of their lives.

It certainly helps to be a morning person because morning is the most important time of the day for the hosts. That is when breakfast is prepared and served. And that is usually when guests avail themselves of the hosts' expertise about the area and plan their day. It is up to the host to decide whether breakfast is served at fixed hours or according to when the guests want to eat. But it is fairly safe to assume that by 10:00 A.M. on weekends, and earlier during the week, a host's breakfast responsibilities are over.

An Opportunity to Get to Know Each Other

In a private-home Bed and Breakfast, interaction with guests varies depending on personal taste. Often, the type of guests who seek out your home have a lot in common with you and have chosen your place because of that. Breakfast style is more varied than in a commercial setting. Sometimes, guests eat in the kitchen while you prepare the meal; other times, they may join you on the porch or alongside the pool. Or if you're in the mood, you may serve breakfast in the dining room on fine china. You have ample opportunity to relax and get to know your guests. Taking care of two couples or even four couples at the breakfast table is relatively easy and is very different from trying to serve different dishes to more than twenty at different times, as the commercial innkeeper must do.

THE B&B INN

So far, I have described differences between a private-home B&B and a commercial inn. In many states, there is something in between: the B&B inn. Usually, this is a place with four to eight rooms, generally in a very tourist-oriented area with few zoning restrictions. It may have a sign outside, and the hosts will often belong to a reservation service but also promote their business themselves. They will serve breakfast, but to their guests only, not to people from the outside. Because of the larger number of rooms, they attempt to keep their occupancy rate high enough to contribute substantially to their income and do regard this as one or both of the hosts' main occupation. It is financially feasible only if the state they are in permits this many rooms without major structural changes to conform to fire and safety codes and the area attracts a high volume of guests with little seasonal variation. Many people who own such inns are retired or semiretired and combine their B&B income earned with pension and investment income.

The table on page 18 will give you an idea of the differences between a private-home B&B, a B&B inn, and a commercial inn.

For those who have the country inn fantasy but don't want the full-time occupation of owning a country inn, becoming a

DIFFERENT TYPES OF FACILITIES

	Private-home B&B	*B&B Inn*	*Commercial Inn*
Number of rooms	1 to 5	5 to 10	Over 10
Open to public	No	Sometimes	Yes
Sign outside	No	Sometimes	Yes
Commercially zoned	No	Sometimes	Yes
Belongs to reservation service	Yes	Yes	Sometimes
Restaurant	No	Guests only	Public
Serves other meals	Not usually	Sometimes	Yes
Has a check-in desk	No	Sometimes	Yes
Must be licensed by state	Not always	Usually	Always
Conforms to restaurant code	Not usually	Sometimes	Always

private-home Bed and Breakfast host may be the answer. Although it is comforting to hear that the average guest will be a middle- to upper-middle-class tourist or business person, hosts often experience some trepidation before their first guest actually walks through the door. But being a B&B host is a far cry from being a hotelier, an altogether different mentality. Remember that it is the private-home ambiance that appeals to the B&B guest. It is the quality of the private home that sets this form of accommodation apart from all others and makes each B&B a unique experience. From a strictly business point of view, operating privately allows hosts to run their business as they wish—picking and choosing guests according to their own standards, selecting dates to take or not take guests, setting house rules, and ultimately deciding how well they wish to get to know their guests.

❖❖❖❖❖❖❖

Question: If I offer B&B in my home, how do I respond to criticism that I am weakening the position of area hotels and motels or competing unfairly with them because I don't have to follow the same rules (such as a restaurant health code)? I wouldn't want to start something that could lead to a decline in local business.

Answer: Although you and the public establishments in your area both provide accommodations for paying guests, lumping together what you do and what they do is neither accurate nor fair. You provide personal hospitality on a prearranged basis. You do not serve the general public. In most states your operation usually does not fall within the purview of the hotel-motel-restaurant code for the simple reason that you are not in that business. With the possible exception of the most popular cities and tourist attractions (where B&B can approach a full-time commitment for a host), you provide accommodations on a limited schedule when it is convenient for you.

Jean Brown, founder of Bed and Breakfast International, San Francisco, America's first reservation service for private homes, stresses to hosts in her network that what they really offer is community service. The benefits to both host and guest extend to the community at large.

> *The publicity B&B receives may encourage travel to an area because it describes friendly hospitality and offers a greater variety of options for people with special needs and interests. It also enables more people to attend events when local hotels are full.*
>
> *Beyond this, short term accommodation in private homes is a needed innovation which many states and local governments encourage because of the economic benefit it brings. The State of Maine, for example, has made a videotape showing how to become a B&B host. Architectural preservationists support B&B as a way to achieve restoration and maintenance of existing*

dwellings which might otherwise become dilapidated due to the rising cost of keeping them in good condition. This is especially true of houses of past eras. There are millions of Americans interested in preserving our unique residential architectural heritage. Older people who may not be physically capable of performing routine maintenance themselves and cannot afford to pay someone else to do it for them, and younger people who find the need for extra income use B&B to pay for restoring an older house they'd love to own and live in. All of this activity adds up to keeping America's older neighborhoods in excellent shape and owner-occupied. B&B's generate fewer occupants and cars than would be the case if a room were permanently rented to a boarder or if a large house were subdivided or turned into condos.

One example of how this works comes immediately to mind. We visited a 73-year-old prospective host, who owned a beautiful home. However, she was beginning to neglect it. Her yard was becoming an eyesore in the neighborhood, and she complained that she could no longer garden because of her arthritis. We sent her guests about eight nights a month. At $30 a night, she earned $240, enough to hire a gardener and do some household repairs. She had reason to keep her house clean as she looked forward to her guests. Her life took on new meaning. On our return visit, she showed us thank-you letters from people all around the world who had stayed with her.

We believe that the B&B movement is a useful and beneficial development in this country. It is an extension of traditional home hospitality and is a property right of the homeowner. City councils, planning boards, and the travel industry should encourage this use of private homes.

Jean takes great pains to distinguish private-home B&B from the operation of a public guesthouse or inn operating illegally in a residential zone. Private-home B&B is self-limiting, she explains, because there are only a few people in each community who have both the interest and the space available to offer the service.

Another factor that keeps B&B a one-to-one business is the time-consuming nature of making custom reservations that match specific hosts with guests who have special needs.

Meeting the needs of people in transition at an affordable cost is a hallmark of B&B everywhere. Here are just a few of the situations in which Bed & Breakfast U.S.A., Ltd., has been able to ease a stressful time for people pulling up their roots.

- *A single manager was transferred by her company to the Albany area. She stayed at a Bed and Breakfast for several months while she started her new position, got oriented to the area, hunted for a house, and waited to move into it.*

- *A European scientist came to America to work on a short-term project for a Rockland County chemical plant. We arranged a stay for him in an apartment in a two-family house owned by one of our hosts. This gave him the convenience of having his own place. His hostess lived in the other part of the house and was available to answer questions about how to get places. When his family came to visit, he used his network membership to stay with them at Bed and Breakfasts in other parts of America.*

- *An English banker came for a two-month stay in New York City. He called us from a $170-a-night hotel. We found him an unhosted garden apartment on the same street as his hotel for $75 a night. His bank saved almost $100 a day, and this guest was much more comfortable.*

- *The Japan Travel Bureau sent a new employee to one of our B&B's so that he would be forced to speak more English. His hosts eased his learning of the language and even helped him get his driver's license.*

- *A sales representative who travels 75 percent of the time started using B&B's. Here is her reaction to her first experience: "I felt so welcome and comfortable in this home. It was the first time I was away that I didn't spend the bulk of the evening on the phone to my family. I sat down to chat with my hosts, got involved in a game of Scrabble, and suddenly it was time for bed. I felt safe and wondered how I had spent so many years staying in cold, impersonal commercial places."*

- A married lawyer started a new position and needed a place to stay while he worked four days a week and began to look for a house. He went home to his family on the weekends. This continued until the end of the school term, when his wife and child were able to join him.

- A California contracting firm was able to submit a lower bid and consequently win a job in Westchester County, New York, because they housed their people at nearby B&B's, saving close to $350 per week per person over housing them at a conventional $85-a-night hotel.

For many women traveling alone or with children, B&B's are a welcome alternative to hotel accommodations. Women appreciate the security, warmth, and friendliness. This may include a light snack before retiring, a friendly chat after a hectic day out, a list of baby-sitters the hosts have used, some special bath salts, an ironing board set up for touching up clothes, laundry facilities, a hall closet well stocked with extra personal grooming and hygiene items, or simply a needle and thread to sew on a stray button. I have often supplied a typewriter to a guest with last-minute changes to make in an important presentation. Although they generally seem more resigned to the inconvenience of traditional forms of travel, men, too, are reporting that B&B makes their time on the road less stressful.

Both men and women appreciate the unpressured environment of a private home. Some women, however, find it especially desirable. They may be worried that in a hotel they will be harassed or receive second-class service in bars or dining rooms. Rather than run that risk, they may wind up ordering meals from room service and watching television, not a pleasant prospect. Often, their families feel better knowing that they are safe and secure in a cozy family home. In my experience, businesswomen report that staying at B&B's makes working away from home much easier. Communities where such accommodations are available are high on preferred assignment lists with executive and management women. As one suburban hostess commented, "B&B here is a women's network. A lot of valuable information is exchanged around my kitchen table over a late-night cup of tea." Looked at in this light, an area's Bed and Breakfast network is an important community asset, an enterprise that attracts people to the area who are likely to explore it while they are there, generating increased revenues for all sorts of businesses.

In an area where there is considerable seasonal fluctuation (such as the skiing or hunting season), there may not be enough off-season business to make a commercial establishment feasible. During the busy season, the B&B network provides an attractive community service, but a host might see only an occasional guest the rest of the year. In other words, Bed and Breakfast complements the rest of the travel industry; it does not supplant it.

❖❖❖❖❖❖

Question: Will I have to take a training program to become a host?

Answer: *There is no formal training program for hosts, but reservation services and adult education centers often spon-*

sor seminars and workshops for prospective hosts and those already in business. These gatherings answer people's initial questions and introduce newcomers to established hosts. Also, professional reservation services always visit potential hosts in their homes and conduct in-depth interviews that give both parties an opportunity to ask all sorts of questions.

This book deals with the most commonly asked questions and situations. It is a compendium of six years' experience in setting up B&B's and reservation services nationally. But, of course, each situation is unique. You will probably want to talk things over with your prospective reservation service well before you take any concrete steps toward opening for business.

A directory of reservation services belonging to Bed & Breakfast Reservation Services Worldwide, all of which adhere to certain standards in conducting business and represent only homes that have been personally inspected by them, is found at the end of this book.

2

Is Bed and Breakfast
for You?

I't is necessary to examine the question of whether Bed and Breakfast is for you from three perspectives: an inventory of your personality and attitudes, how your family reacts to the prospect of opening your home to paying guests, what, and how realistic, your expectations are.

Complete the checklist on page 26 to find out if your personality and attitudes are similar to those of successful hosts.

Though there is no such thing as the perfect host, there are certain attributes or personal characteristics that make it more likely for someone to enjoy hosting. If your answer to most of the preceding characteristics was yes, you are probably good host material.

The B&B hosts I have met are between the ages of twenty-five and eighty-three; are single, married, divorced, widowed; active at professional careers, at home with children, or retired. In other words, it is personality rather than any particular demographic characteristics that the hosts have in common. Successful hosts are interesting people, usually satisfied with their lives, proud of their homes, and convinced that they live in one of the best possible places. Because of their enthusiasm for home and community they are able to share an insider's view with guests.

Characteristics of a Successful Host	Yes	No	Willing to Change
Knows and appreciates community and region	——	——	——
Is enthusiastic about meeting new people	——	——	——
Enjoys preparing for entertaining	——	——	——
Can sense ordinary needs of others	——	——	——
Can take risks	——	——	——
Likes keeping home in good order	——	——	——
Has a wide range of interests	——	——	——
Sees others as generally trustworthy	——	——	——
Can get excited about the interests of others	——	——	——
Is accustomed to having company at home	——	——	——
Communicates directly and diplomatically	——	——	——
Organizes time and schedules realistically	——	——	——
Infuses home with personality and comfort	——	——	——
Allows others the privacy they desire	——	——	——
Pays attention to details but is not fussy	——	——	——
Maintains significant nonbusiness friendships	——	——	——
Is flexible, can roll with the punches	——	——	——
Has a good sense of humor	——	——	——
A family free of alcohol or drug problems	——	——	——

BE THE REALTOR'S ALLY

This enthusiasm is one reason that realtors suggest B&B's to out-of-town buyers as a base from which to see the community and select a home. The host, often unknowingly, becomes a representative for the community. The fact that the host has enjoyed raising a family there suggests to potential residents that they will also enjoy living there. Since he or she is not selling anything, the host is not seen as having a vested interest in any sale and is therefore sometimes taken more seriously than the realtor.

YOUR FAMILY'S REACTION

How your family reacts to the prospect of opening your home is a very important part of your decision to proceed. Instant agreement and enthusiasm are not necessary. Often, because of ignorance or a difference in expectations about what a B&B will entail, family members are reluctant at first. It is essential to have discussions about what will really be expected of each person. Let your family read this book or sit in on a seminar on hosting.

Consider who will receive the money generated by the B&B and what this money will be used for. In England, my husband and I stayed at a B&B run by a banker, his wife, and three young children. It seemed to us that the wife, who had no outside job, did most of the work (cleaning and breakfast preparation). The husband worked in London and left for his office each day before we awoke. He was quite warm to us on the weekend, however, and made us feel very welcome. The three children shared one room during our stay so that two of their bedrooms were available for guests. Our hostess told us that this was a family project. They take guests only during six weeks of the summer travel season. The money they earn permits the family to enjoy a wonderful holiday on an island off the coast of Spain for the last two weeks of the summer.

If you live alone, of course, the decision is all yours. Nevertheless, you should be prepared to deal with the reaction of your friends and relatives. Children long grown and on their own often expect that when they return home for a family Thanksgiving or Christmas holiday, the room of their childhood memories will wait for them. It is sometimes necessary to remind these grown children that they now have homes and children of their own and that what was once their room has been redone in the decor of your choice.

If the last of your flock is away at school, it is appropriate to offer that room to B&B guests, but you will probably have to redecorate it to welcome adults. It can't look as though a teenage son or daughter could take up residence at a moment's notice. If you have fixed up one room for B&B and guests are coming with children, a room complete with posters of rock stars on the walls could appropriately be offered at a reduced price for the youngsters in the party. I will address more of the home requirements in Chapter 3.

If you live alone, family and friends may also be concerned that it may not be safe for you to take in strangers. You can reassure them in a number of ways. Explain that you will be accepting guests only through a reservation service that has screened them. Some hostesses who live alone feel more comfortable accepting only women, couples, or families. Rest assured that many singles own Bed and Breakfasts and have only positive experiences.

Awkward Situations

In most cases, one member of the host couple or family is more involved in the business than the others. This is fine as long as the others are not openly hostile to the idea or the guests or unwilling to help out in a pinch. Problems develop in situations where one person feels forced to participate despite a strong objection to the venture. I know of only three cases where such a conflict has caused the hosts to close their B&B. One involved a young couple who had traveled widely and enjoyed meeting people the world over. Their home had two rooms and a bath on a separate floor. Conditions seemed ideal for a B&B. But the husband had grown up in a series of foster homes and soon found that having visitors in the house touched off too many painful memories of his past. Although all the guests were wonderful, he felt strongly that he could not continue. His wife, despite feeling that the experience was wonderfully enriching to their lives, agreed, and they closed their business.

In the second case, a well-liked hostess had asked our reservation service to send as many guests as possible; she loved the whole experience and wanted to see if she could make a financial success of her venture. Indeed, she started having guests every weekend and during the week as well and was thriving on the stimulation and feeling of a job well done. Guests always gave her rave reviews, and I was totally surprised when she stopped by the office to say that she could no longer take guests. What was the problem? She explained that the more business she did, the more her husband resented the attention she paid the guests. He became increasingly withdrawn when guests were there and hostile when they were a few moments late to the breakfast table. Although he knew that his wife loved her business and wouldn't force her to stop, he couldn't disguise his feelings, and she stopped on her own.

The third case involved a lovely B&B that had been in business for three years. When the hosts began, their ten-year-old daughter was very helpful and enjoyed the attention of the guests. By thirteen, however, she was experiencing adolescent growing pains, and she viewed the guests as unwanted intruders. Her negative attitude toward them made her mother uncomfortable, and the family chose to stop taking guests. But they plan to resume when their daughter passes through this phase or goes off to college.

Luckily, the financial investment of using a home as a B&B is usually minimal, and hosts can continue for as long as it seems right and they enjoy it.

Often hosts are fearful until they have had their first guest. With each guest thereafter, they become more comfortable and confident. They realize that they can expect the majority of guests to be lovely people. You meet an occasional pill, but B&B guests are a pretty terrific breed.

Family Members Help Each Other

My husband, George, a technical author and editor, is often more comfortable with books and figures than with people. He is not normally outgoing but really enjoys the opportunity that B&B affords him to get to know people on his own turf. Although he is helpful when asked, he often schedules racquetball at 9:00 A.M. on Saturday, leaving me to take care of the guests. B&B works for us because I don't mind this. If I have to be away, he magically becomes the epitome of the gracious host and doesn't mind doing so because it is not expected of him on a regular basis. My daughter, now eight, has met people from all over the world and flourished in her interaction with them. She wants to learn languages and plans to travel when she gets old enough to see the world. As she has grown up and become more capable, I have asked her to do some of the chores related to keeping the house neat, stripping the beds, and setting the table. I always make sure that she knows that the money earned by having guests enables us to enjoy a more comfortable life and do more things.

YOUR EXPECTATIONS

If your personality fits that of other successful hosts, and if your family and friends are supportive, and your timing seems right, it is important to know what you expect to get from the B&B experience. For most hosts, although the extra income or tax benefits play a part, the joy of meeting the guests is always paramount.

The Joys of Hosting

The influx of guests from all over the world can bring great cultural enrichment to your home and family. Here are a few examples from my own experience.

A group of Japanese men came to the Croton Clearwater Revival, an annual music and crafts event that celebrates the Hudson River and its cleanup. When they made their reservation, they learned that we had a four-year-old child. They came with gifts for each member of the family, but the most special were the presents for Cydney. On Monday, she went off to "show and tell" at nursery school with a brightly colored cloth that ties in the corners, the Japanese version of the paper bag. Inside it were all kinds of paper animals and balloons and other children's toys. She was able to tell her fascinated classmates the Japanese name of each item and a story to go with it. For that day at least, Cydney was the most cosmopolitan child in her class.

On another occasion, our guests were a concert pianist and a concert violinist. They had chosen our place because we have a piano. Each night, after they returned from supper, they would ask whether we minded if they played. We were treated to wonderful concerts in the comfort of our own living room. We heard fascinating tales of their travels to perform in Europe and got a firsthand account of a totally different life-style.

An appraiser and his wife who were very interested in Croton's rich artistic history stayed over a weekend. We took them on a little tour of the town, describing the various people who have lived here and some of the architecturally interesting buildings and sites. One of these was the Croton Dam. Months later, at Christmastime, we received a large envelope from them containing an 1889 *Scientific American* with a photograph of the Croton Dam on the front. In the enclosed note, this couple told us they had enjoyed their stay with us so much that they wanted to repay us in some way for the extras we had shared with them.

Clifford, an IBM employee, stayed with us for a few days. He had just started what proved to be a long-term assignment at the company's research center (ten minutes from our home) and needed a place four nights a week for about three months. He lived a little over two hours away and would go home each weekend. Our daily rate was more expensive than he could pay, so we arranged a prorated weekly price in exchange for some yard work three hours a week. This proved to be mutually beneficial because he loved to work out the frustrations of his day pruning the hedges and weeding the garden. I really got a double benefit; often when George came home, he felt guilty seeing Clifford already hard at work and was inspired to help out. Clifford's assignment was extended twice, and his stay with us went on for nearly ten months. This guest became a trusted friend who even baby-sat for us on those evenings when we had scheduling conflicts.

What Do Guests Expect of a Host?

Guests have expectations, too. At the very least, they expect a clean and pleasant room, access to the public areas of your home (television room, yard, and the like), and a hearty American breakfast. And they will expect you to be available to answer questions about the area and to give them the benefit of your insider's expertise.

A good host sizes up guests and within a few moments after their arrival has a good idea what to offer to make them feel welcome and settle in. Remember, you are in the hospitality business and that means personal service. Do what you would do for a friend or relative who has come to stay. If the weather is warm, offer a cold drink; if it's cold, offer something hot. Some guests will bring their own wine or liquor so that they can have drinks in their room before heading out to dine. These guests need glasses and an ice-filled bucket. While showing guests their room, experienced hosts offer to send up ice. Keep tourist information and local maps (photocopies are okay) in the room. Hosts who provide these materials allow guests to learn preliminary things about the area for themselves. By the time the guests approach the host, they will be asking more specific questions, which are usually much easier to answer than a vague question such as, "What's there to do around here?" It helps to keep an up-to-date newspaper listing local movies and events so that you can let guests know what's happening in the area, what time things start, and whether reservations are necessary. If you know that something is coming to town that guests may want to attend, mention it on the phone when they call for directions so that you can get tickets or make reservations for them. Your guests rely on you to be informative. After all, they may be coming from a distance and not realize that unless they plan ahead, they may arrive to find the event or best seats sold out.

Collect menus from local restaurants to give guests a chance to see both selection and price before they make reservations. I often call the restaurant for them to ensure that the restaurant knows that they are coming as a result of my efforts. It is always good to have the support of other businesses in the community. They may even be a source of new guests.

The guest room must be clean, with fresh sheets on the bed and clean towels. Guests who stay a few days are expected to make their own beds. Fresh towels should be given every few days, or the guest should be told to ask for them when needed or take them from a linen closet or other cabinet. Whichever way you do this is up to you. The main point is, of course, that the guest must know that you are available to see that his or her needs are met. If a guest stays more than a week, he or she should be informed of your room-cleaning schedule so that personal items will be removed from dresser surfaces and the like to enable you to clean properly. Beds should be changed and the room thoroughly cleaned, just as you would for members of your own family.

Bathrooms need daily maintenance. If guests share a bath, hosts should glance in whenever they pass by and wipe down surfaces; check the sink, tub, and bowl; and make sure that there is adequate toilet tissue, soap, and facial tissue. Wastebaskets in the rooms and bath should be emptied daily.

The public areas of your home and the kitchen should be kept sparkling clean, neat, and company-ready. This may sound like a burden, but most B&B families find that having a clean home is one of the extra benefits of taking in guests. Too many of us allow routine chores to get away from us when our busy lives focus our attention outside the home. With this type of home-based business, the need to keep the house looking attractive stops you from allowing a mess to accumulate.

A hearty American breakfast usually includes bacon, eggs, bread, juice, and coffee, or equivalent. Only your imagination limits the variety that can be offered here. (See Chapter 9, "Best Breakfasts," for some suggestions.) Just remember that no one should leave your table hungry. In some states, hosts are prohibited from serving foods prepared at home and must resort to packaged foods. This is disappointing to many guests and should, therefore, be explained in advance. Whether you set a breakfast hour or arrange breakfast according to your guests' schedules is up to you, but it should be clearly stated in any material written and distributed about your home. It is an unhappy guest who sleeps past the breakfast hour, especially if he or she was not told about it beforehand.

Some of your guests will arrive wanting total privacy and will retreat to their room; others will want company or be interested in hearing about the particulars of your restoration or decorating efforts or lots of detail about what there is to do nearby. A successful host responds to these various needs, always realizing that the guests are not there to amuse the hosts. Good hosts also balance their own needs for privacy and free time with their interest in meeting new people.

It is important to have integrity and not permit people to make you do more than you feel comfortable doing. Making exceptions as special favors often causes problems. It is therefore necessary to think through beforehand what you will and won't be willing to do for guests. Here are some things that fall into this category.

1. Will you pick guests up at the train or airport? If you do this, how will they be able to get around on their own? Does this mean you will have to provide other meals if they can't walk to a restaurant?

2. Do you want to supply other meals? Routinely? Only for singles? Only on holidays? Only when asked to ahead of time?

3. Can guests smoke in your home? Do you smoke? (It's hard to tell others they can't if you do.) Would you be comfortable with smoking restricted to certain rooms? What about cigars or pipes?

4. How much notice do you need before a guest comes? Are you comfortable with last-minute calls? If not, let your reservation service know, and be firm. Running around trying to prepare for an arrival on short notice can cause some people to become so frazzled that they make a poor impression on the guests they have gone out of their way for.

5. What if someone asks to bring a pet? If you have a pet, how is it likely to react? What if the visiting pet brings fleas or ticks into your home?

6. If a guest is going to arrive late, how do you handle it? If you are in a ski area, late arrivals on Friday night are often part of doing business, especially if you have a two-night minimum stay on weekends. In other areas, you may well examine your normal bedtime and be firm about guests arriving by a certain hour. Often, a guest can stop by during the day to get a key, and then it doesn't matter what time they come back at night. Some hosts have a combination lock on the door. The combination can be changed regularly to maintain a feeling of security, but guests can be told the combination if the hosts know that they are arriving after bedtime. Sometimes, it's best to tell people to stay one night at a motel and come up in the morning. You are the best judge of this. It can be very aggravating to wait up until 1:00 A.M. for a guest who promised to arrive at 11:00 and then calls at 11:30 to say he or she had been delayed. The main thing to remember is that you are a private-home B&B, not a hotel with twenty-four-hour staff and round-the-clock check-in.

7. What about children? If you have children and lots of baby equipment, swings, and childproof locks on your kitchen cabinets, you will probably welcome families with young children. It is my experience that people who go to B&B's with children usually have well-behaved youngsters. If it has been a long time since children came to your home and the presence of your crystal collection on the coffee table makes you cringe at the thought of a toddler, you may want to restrict your guests to children above six. If your goal is to offer B&B only to romantic couples who might find it distracting to share the breakfast table with anyone in a high chair, you may want to limit your home to adults. You can do this because you are operating a private-home B&B. If you were running an inn or other public accommoda-

tions, you would have to abide by the law that prohibits discrimination by age.

8. Do you want to let a guest have a wedding on your property? What would this entail? Would it cause parking problems or trouble with neighbors? If you want to do this, what should you charge?

THE SCOPE OF YOUR INVOLVEMENT

You must decide how large a role B&B will play in your life. You may open one room or many. You may take guests only a few days a month or as often as guests want to come. You may be available only for festivals or football games at the nearby college, graduation week, or other times when there is a shortage of accommodations in your area. You can accept the money for yourself or donate it to a favorite charity or religious group.

It is sometimes prudent to begin on a small scale, fixing up one or two rooms, and then expand the amount of your home available to guests as demand warrants. As your business grows, realize that it is necessary to plan personal vacations in advance. Whether you get someone to be host in your stead or just stop taking guests, don't be talked out of taking your time off because a houseful of guests wants you personally. Everyone needs occasional R and R from B&B.

❖❖❖❖❖❖❖

Question: My husband and I have traveled in Europe and enjoyed our stays in everything from Italian *pensiones* to French *chateaux* and Swiss village *zimmers*. We'd like to become involved with Bed and Breakfast in our area, but we don't like the idea of putting up a sign or distributing leaflets to just anyone through the local tourist information center. Our privacy and personal security mean a lot to us—and to our neighborhood. Any solution?

Answer: *Your concerns are typical of most newcomers to hosting in this country. In fact, American-style Bed and Breakfast owes its particular form to them. By far the overwhelming majority of B&B's in North America operate with no overt commercialism whatever. In most cases, there is no sign to set apart the B&B from any other residence on the street. Guests are prescreened either by the host or, more commonly, by a professional reservation service to which the host belongs.*

You usually know weeks ahead of time who is coming, their employment, their home address, their telephone number, their bank or their credit card number, their reason for coming to your area, whether they are past customers of the reservation service, how long they will stay, their dietary restriction (if any), and whether they will require any special assistance.

You are in the hospitality service business, and your guests will generally be the kind of visitors any community would welcome. Indeed, a very large part of hosting involves providing guests with access to the community that is simply unavailable at a reasonable price (some would say at any price) from the commercial hotel and motel industry. In many instances, your guests will be already known in the area. They may be about to move there permanently because of a job change, may be coming to see a new grandchild, or may be back for a class reunion or in town for a professional meeting. Some are doing precollege interviews, are staying close to a relative in a hospital or nursing home, are members of a wedding party, or are representing a local business in a legal matter.

Most guests stay more than one night, and most have a specific agenda. Many will have a reason to return in the future or to recommend you to friends and associates heading your way. After you have been operating awhile, you will find that word of mouth means a great deal.

Balancing your need for privacy and security with your interest in meeting new people and supplementing your income is one of the basic issues I discuss in this book. Bed and Breakfast is consistent with other occupations traditional in residential neighborhoods (e.g., accountant, doctor, piano teacher, computer or typing service) and generates less traffic than most of these. For the most part, hosting is so unobtrusive that until you inform them, your neighbors might not even notice!

❖❖❖❖❖❖❖

Question: I work full time, and we have an active household (three school-age children). It would be impossible for me to be at home all the time to take reservations and wait for guests to arrive. Should I stop thinking about becoming a host?

Answer: *Most hosts lead full lives. Unlike an inn, motel, club, or resort, your home is private. You set the limits and house rules. You advise your reservation service of your booking preferences (spelled out to them when they first visit your home) so that only those guests meeting your specifications will be matched to you. This information includes dates when you want to have guests and whether you will accept smokers, young children, unmarried couples, members of the opposite sex, or pets. You are not obliged to accept any other categories of guests. This screening and matching is one of the major reasons to join a reservation service.*

The reservation service also takes care of your reservations and cancellations. A guest who has made confirmed reservations through your service typically contacts you by telephone a few days ahead of time to arrange a mutually convenient arrival time. You are not expected to sit there waiting all day. You are extending your hospitality as you would for any other invited guest. Clearly, you are not signing up to be-

come a servant at the beck and call of anyone who chooses to knock on your door. B&B is highly flexible; simply notify your reservation service when you do not wish to receive guests. This can apply to vacations, certain days of the week when you work or have other appointments, or any other time when you just want to relax. The advent of reservation services in most parts of America has considerably simplified the business end for hosts opening their homes for B&B.

❖❖❖❖❖❖❖

Question: What makes your reservation service reject a B&B?

Answer: In general, I look for a pleasant setting, a convenient location, and a warm and gracious host. I cannot accept people who are only interested in the money, whose homes are shabby, or who appear to be so lonely that their guests will be expected to entertain them.

For example, here is the story of a home I rejected because the host lacked both trust and the ability to put herself in the guests' shoes.

A woman from Rockland County, New York, called to discuss opening a B&B. After a lengthy conversation, I sent her an application, and she sent back pictures of a beautiful estate that is on the National Register of Historic Homes. She was very excited about the prospect of becoming a host. We arranged a date for the home visit, and I told her that I would be arriving at noon. In response, she told me not to get out of the car if the dog was in the yard when I arrived. I informed her that I was no longer coming. Anyone who allows vicious attack dogs to run loose when she knows that guests are arriving is not ready to welcome strangers. I am well acquainted with the area and would certainly have arrived on time, but guests who are new to the area may misjudge their time and arrive early or late. My reservation service has a stake in assuring guests that they can reasonably expect to arrive with all limbs intact.

❖❖❖❖❖❖❖

Question: My husband is away a great deal on business. One of my good friends is widowed. Another is divorced and has a teenage daughter living with her. We all have nice homes that we are proud of, not historically significant or anything, but comfortable. And we have spare time. Would we qualify as B&B hosts?

Answer: *Most B&B hosts are women. If there are other family members involved, they usually play supporting roles, pitching in as needed. You and your friends might be ideal candidates, assuming you enjoy making people comfortable and do not need to rely on the money you will earn from B&B to maintain your life-style. The greatest skill you will need is the ability to be a gracious host who takes pride in her personal achievements.*

Most hosts have invested a lot of themselves in their homes, are accustomed to dealing with people who have professional backgrounds, have a variety of interest, and are sure enough of themselves not to allow others to take advantage of their good nature and good will. They also become experts on their community or region, welcome spur-of-the-moment entertaining, might consider inviting visitors to participate in some family activities, and gain satisfaction and pleasure from meeting the needs of others. The most successful B&B's combine the attractions of a comfortable home, a willing host, and a desirable location. Without a genial host, the most intriguing house in the most stylish vacation spot will have a short career as a B&B. To decide for yourselves if you want to take the next step, you and your friends can start by reading this book and spending some weekends at B&B's to experience what it is like to be a guest as well as to learn firsthand from some experienced hosts.

3

Evaluating Your Home's Assets and Liabilities

One of the joys of B&B is the chance it offers to sample other life-styles as well as other locales. My reservation service, Bed & Breakfast U.S.A., Ltd., offers accommodations in diverse settings. For example, a fifty-two-foot yacht anchored in Long Island Sound, a dairy farm overlooking the Mohawk River, a mansion near Saratoga, a working farm with a cow named Ma, lakeside cottages in the Catskills, a loft with a waterbed in a solar-heated contemporary-style house near Albany, and an apartment, complete with doorman, in a Manhattan luxury high-rise.

It is very important for hosts to realize that when a commercial facility puts the words "Bed and Breakfast" or "Complimentary Breakfast" on its marquee, that doesn't make it a B&B. It is the noncommercial qualities that are most essential. A commercial place has staff that comes on and off in eight-hour shifts. The person who says "hello" is seldom the one who says "good-bye." Not so at your home. Your guests' enjoyment or dissatisfaction is your direct responsibility. It is therefore in everyone's best interest for you to take a good hard look at what you have to offer.

RATING YOUR HOME

The B&B life is not only for those with property of extravagant beauty or opulence, though, of course such B&B's are perennially popular. For the business traveler, a suburban split-level with all the comforts of home and a location down the road from corporate headquarters may be just the thing. There is no set prescription for the perfect host, and there is no single type of home that meets all needs or suits all tastes. It takes only a short time to realize how much success depends on diversity, the incredible mix of people, occupations, interests, and locales that make up our society. Whereas the hotel and motel industry has adopted a cookie-cutter approach to most of its establishments, B&B thrives on offering only absolute originals, unique combination of hosts and homes.

Although B&B accommodations can be offered in many different home settings, it is imperative that prospective guests be accurately informed about what you have to offer. For a realistic estimate of how much business you might do and as an aid in pricing your room(s) sensibly, compare your accommodations with this checklist of typical features for standard, executive, and deluxe accommodations. (Your reservation service will also help you to do this.)

Feature	Is This Your Home?
STANDARD (minimum requirements for a B&B)	
Usually convenient to some desired attraction	_____
Shared bath (sometimes with host family)	_____
Sleeping room kept ready for use (clean, aired, neat)	_____
Kitchen and other public areas kept company-ready	_____
Guest room outfitted with the following basic comforts:	_____
• Two pillows	_____
• Firm mattress	_____

43

Feature	Is This Your Home?
• Mattress pad	_____
• Two sets of sheets	_____
• Extra blankets	_____
• Soft, fluffy towels (two sets)	_____
• Room-darkening curtains or shades	_____
• Reading lamp by bed	_____
• Clock radio	_____
• Towel rack	_____
• At least two empty drawers in bureau	_____
• At least half of a closet	_____

EXECUTIVE (includes all features of *standard*, plus)

Generally a grander house with more rooms	_____
May have historical or architectural interest	_____
Usually has quality furniture	_____
Guest room(s) share bath separate from hosts'	_____
Usually convenient to businesses or attractions	_____
Has some special amenities for guests' use:	
• Library	_____
• Sitting room	_____
• Fireplace	_____
• Pool	_____
• Garden	_____
• Hot tub	_____
• Sauna	_____

- Views   _____

- Stable   _____

- Access to clubs (tennis, swimming, golf, yacht)   _____

- Host shares hobbies (weaving, bridge, restoring antique cars, outlet shopping)   _____

- Waterfront   _____

- Piano   _____

- Kitchenette   _____

- Jacuzzi   _____

- Exercise equipment   _____

- Office equipment (computer, typewriter)   _____

- Sports equipment (bicycles, croquet set, volleyball)   _____

- Videocassette recorder   _____

- Darkroom or art studio   _____

- Collectibles   _____

- Sewing room   _____

- Music room or sound system   _____

DELUXE (includes many features of *executive*, plus)

- Usually a historic or otherwise noteworthy property in top condition   _____

- More likely to have private guest bath   _____

- Expensive furnishings (custom decor)   _____

- Variety of amenities   _____

- Gourmet breakfast (possibly in bed)   _____

- May not be conveniently situated but is so interesting that people will want to visit   _____

- Antique or luxury linens   _____

Feature	Is This Your Home?
• Fine china and crystal	_____
• Separate quarters for guests (cottage, carriage house, pool house)	_____
• May have staff in addition to host	_____

You may notice that none of these categories mentioned any particular number of rooms. In fact, B&B's in each category may have only one room set aside for guests. Quantity is not the same as quality. Some guests prefer the charm of a very small place where they can really get to know the host family; others prefer a larger place where the mix of guests from all over the country or the world will add enjoyment to their stay.

YOUR LOCATION

How much demand is there in your area for overnight lodging?

Is this demand constant?

Is it seasonal?

Is it related to events at a local college or other institution?

Are there any tourist attractions nearby?

Do they have special events?

Are there any local festivals that occur every year?

Are there any wineries?

Are there any large businesses?

What hotels and motels are within ten minutes drive?

Within twenty minutes?

Within thirty minutes?

What are their capacities and rates?

How often do you notice No Vacancy signs?

How far are you from a large city whose residents may be looking for weekend getaways?

Is there skiing nearby?

Will guests be able to arrive by public transportation and get around without a car?

Are there other B&B's in your area?

How are they doing?

How does your place compare with them?

In answering the preceding questions, you are getting a good idea about the desirability of your location. If you are near a large city or corporate area, your location will be more interesting to business guests, the Monday-through-Friday crowd. Tourist traffic is more seasonal; guests are typically getting away for a weekend or staying at a B&B en route to a long vacation. The vacation season depends on the part of the country you are in. North of the Mason-Dixon line, is usually considered April through October. In the Sun Belt, the season may be the reverse. Maine offers a spectacular seacoast and lots of tourist attractions but a limited season. Most traffic to Maine is in July and August. The difference between the cost of a house in Maine and that of one in Massachusetts is enormous. The difference in seasonal demand will be similar. If you are under two hours driving time from a major city, guests can get there for a two-day weekend and still have time to enjoy the area. A drive time of more than two hours is usually considered too long for anything less than a three-day trip.

In the travel industry, some places are considered final destinations, and others are stopping points along the way. Maine, for example, is considered a final destination; like Alaska, it is not usually considered as being on the way to anywhere else. Massachusetts, on the other hand, might be either a final destination or a stop on the way to Maine, Canada, Vermont, or New Hampshire.

Remember, your B&B is likely to have under five rooms for guests. If ten couples want to stay on any particular night, you will have to turn five of them away. If a festival is in town and 100 couples want to stay, you will still have only five rooms and will have to turn the rest away. Of course, you can bet that on weekends of high demand in your region, you will have a full house. But what you should be most interested in is how many times demand outstrips supply in your area, not how great occasional demand will be. You can be sure that if there were high demand in your area on a constant basis, more hotel and motel rooms would be built. Commercial facilities have to pay overhead year-round and can't survive on sporadic periods of high demand. But you can as long as your expectations are realistic.

Once you have answered the preceding two lists of questions, you should have a good idea about the desirability of both your location and your home. Demand for your accommodations can be judged on the basis of these two factors. Remember, a standard B&B in a desirable location may do more business than a deluxe B&B in a remote location.

TAKE A GOOD LOOK AT YOUR HOME

First Impressions

Your guests' first impression of your home will be formed as they drive up to your home. What will they see? Is there any repair work, painting, or yard work that needs to be done?

48

Would flower-filled window boxes or better-trimmed hedges make your home more inviting? Can your house number be seen from the street? The last thing you want is for a late-arriving guest to wake up your neighbors.

When I was a small child, my parents bought a waterfront home in Larchmont, New York. It was a big move for them, and much deliberation and numerous visits were necessary before they made up their mind. The odd thing about visiting this house was that sometimes the owner would only be available to show it in the morning, but at other times, she was only available in the afternoon. What we didn't realize was that she was available when the tide was high. At low tide, the house backed on a cove of mud twelve feet down, not the most appealing sight. This taught me that because first impressions mean so much, you should show off your house to its best advantage. If you are giving directions and there are two ways to approach your home, send your guests by the most scenic route even if it is not the fastest or the most direct. Later you can tell them about shortcuts. If they are arriving after dark, have the house well lit. Make their welcome warm and inviting. In the winter, for example, a fire burning in the fireplace makes a house seem cozy.

The Interior

Walk through the public rooms of your house, and look at them as a stranger would. What do you see? What feeling do you get? Are there repairs to be made? Is something frayed or broken? Should it be fixed, replaced, or simply put away? What will it cost in time and money to make these changes? Look at each of the potential guest rooms. Are they large or small? What type of beds do they have? Will you need new furniture? Will you have to redecorate? Should you start by fixing up one room and see what comes of it? These are some of the questions you should be asking yourself. If any of the answers are yes, you will want to examine your rooms in more detail. If some changes need to be made, the questions that follow will help you determine how much work needs to be done, how long it will take, and what it will cost.

The Guest Rooms

Before you offer a room to a guest, make sure to sleep in it first. You need to find out firsthand what else needs to be done.

CHECKLIST

Do the shades block out the early morning sun? _____

Is the temperature comfortable? _____

Will you need to adjust the thermostat in this portion of the house? _____

Will a fan or air-conditioner be necessary come summer? _____

Are there extra blankets in the closet? _____

Is the bed comfortable? Is it long enough for a tall person? _____

Are the bedsprings too noisy? _____

Do the windows and screens work easily? _____

Are the pillows comfortable, not too hard or too soft? _____

Is the air circulation good, no musty smells or stuffy closet? _____

Do the dresser drawers slide in and out easily? _____

Is the reading light good to read by, not too bright or too dim? _____

Are there enough hangers in the closet? _____

What sounds do you hear? _____

The last question is especially important because most people sleep on one side of a house for years and aren't aware that other bedrooms may not be as quiet as theirs. Rooms at the front of the house may be less desirable on days when the garbage men arrive at 6:00 A.M. to pick up the trash. For example, I visited a home near Cooperstown, New York, and was shown to a beautiful, well-appointed room where I slept soundly. Early the next morning, however, I was awakened by the sound of a rush of running water behind my head. It turned out that the shower pipes were in the wall at the head of the bed; when the host's son got up early to shower before school, the running water and clanging pipes were enough to rudely awaken any sleeping guest. It was quite a startling experience.

When I mentioned this to the hostess, she said, "Oh, I forgot to tell you. The room just doesn't look as good if the furniture is arranged differently. There are too many doors and windows to move the bed from that spot." My advice was to utilize this room last, to rearrange the furniture even if it isn't the nicest way artistically, and to ask the young man to shower before retiring. I also suggested that if all the other rooms were booked, she should warn guests that this room backs on the bathroom and that they may hear the sound of running water. In this way, guests will take the room knowing its drawback and won't be frightened by the noise.

You will find that guests who are told about your home's weaknesses as well as its assets won't complain if those shortcomings cause minor inconvenience. For example, a very old house may have a small hot water tank. Until you are able to get a larger one, share this problem with guests so that some will shower at night and others in the morning.

Here are other examples: Guests staying at homes along the Hudson River all want to enjoy the river view. They need to be told that the railroad line was built at the river's edge and that in any home from which they can see the river they can also hear the train. If you work outside your home and must leave early, don't accept guests who don't know this. A guest who awakens at 10:00 A.M. surprised to find a note from a host who has left for the office will be very dissatisfied. But a guest who has accepted the accommodation knowing that breakfast is served at 7:00 A.M. and that late risers must prepare their own meal will do it in good spirit.

The Bathroom

Use the guest bathroom, too.

Is the bathroom clean and shiny? _____

Is extra lighting or a flashlight necessary to get there after dark? _____

Does the tub drain well? _____

Are the cleaning things and extra toilet paper handy? _____

Is the water temperature appropriate? _____

Does the door lock work properly? _____

Safety and Comfort

Here are more questions to ask yourself as you evaluate guest accommodations.

Points to Check	Date	Professional to Call
Smoke detector installed in each guest room	_____	_____
Smoke detector in hallway(s)	_____	_____
Smoke detector in kitchen	_____	_____
Nonskid pads under throw rugs	_____	_____
Night-light for hallway(s)	_____	_____

52

Night-light for bathroom   _____   _____

Adequate outdoor lighting   _____   _____

House number visible at night   _____   _____

Secure pool fencing   _____   _____

Bushes, vines, and other plants
    trimmed back from walkways   _____   _____

Escape ladder (collapsible) for
    second-floor bedrooms if needed _____   _____

Fire escape rehearsal   _____   _____

Fire escape map   _____   _____

Nonskid treads on outdoor steps
    (or textured paint to improve
    footings)   _____   _____

Secure pet restraints and fencing
    as needed   _____   _____

Child/toddler stair gates as needed _____   _____

Flashlights in sleeping rooms
    (with working batteries)   _____   _____

Eight-hour supply of candles in
    case of power failure   _____   _____

Air-conditioner or fan in working
    order   _____   _____

Several run-throughs with any new
    kitchen equipment (especially
    microwave oven)   _____   _____

Fireplace(s) cleaned   _____   _____

Fireplace(s) inspected for flue
    problems   _____   _____

Ample supply of kindling and wood   _____   _____

Appropriately sized fireplace
    screen(s)   _____   _____

Fire extinguisher for each room   _____   _____

Points to Check	Date	Professional to Call
List of emergency telephone numbers placed next to phones	_____	_____
Items needed by family members removed from guest rooms	_____	_____
Hot water temperature checked	_____	_____
Hot water availability adequate for family and full number of guests (check number of showers possible before water cools. Can you run washer or dishwater without affecting hot water supply to showers?)	_____	_____
Water-saving devices installed	_____	_____
Bed slept in by you to check comfort	_____	_____
Extra bed space for children as needed (high riser, trundle, inflatable mattress, rollaways, cot, futon)	_____	_____
Privacy locks on bedroom and bathroom doors above reach of small children	_____	_____
Grab bar installed on wall beside bath tub	_____	_____
Wastebaskets in bedroom and bath	_____	_____
At poolside		
• Life jackets	_____	_____
• Water wings	_____	_____
• Pole	_____	_____
• Life preserver	_____	_____
• Garbage pail	_____	_____
• Scooper for pet droppings	_____	_____

Guest closet extras

- Bathrobes or pool cover-ups _____ _____
- Hair dryer (or in bathroom) _____ _____
- Curling iron (or in bathroom) _____ _____
- Hot rollers (or in bathroom) _____ _____
- Sewing kit _____ _____
- Iron (may be in hall closet) _____ _____
- Ironing board (may be in hall closet) _____ _____
- Small refrigerator (optional) _____ _____
- Electric hot water device (optional) _____ _____
- Padded hangers (optional) _____ _____
- Wooden hangers (at least twelve) _____ _____
- Sunscreen or sunblock cream (may be in bathroom) _____ _____
- Plastic glasses and dishes (optional) _____ _____
- Paper napkins (optional) _____ _____
- Vase _____ _____
- Candles and matches _____ _____
- Sachet or potpourri (optional) _____ _____
- Neck pillow (optional) _____ _____

In the bathroom

Tile and grouting scrubbed to remove and prevent mildew _____ _____

Bathtub, sink, and toilet bowl scrubbed _____ _____

Shower curtain scrubbed with vinyl cleaner _____ _____

Points to Check	Date	Professional to Call
Shower stall and floor scrubbed	_____	_____
Drains unclogged and treated with a drain cleaner	_____	_____
Automatic toilet bowl cleaner installed	_____	_____
Decals (nonskid) installed in bottom of tub or shower	_____	_____
Bath mat with nonskid backing	_____	_____
Windows and mirrored surfaces cleaned	_____	_____
Metal fixtures shined	_____	_____
Towel rack and shower curtain rod tightly secured	_____	_____
Full-length mirror installed on back of door	_____	_____
Bathroom cabinet or closet stocked with:		
• Paper cups	_____	_____
• Tissues	_____	_____
• Extra toilet paper	_____	_____
• Liquid soap (by sink)	_____	_____
• Bar soap (in shower or tub)	_____	_____
• Air freshener	_____	_____
• Hand lotion	_____	_____
• Band-Aids	_____	_____
• Cotton swabs	_____	_____
• Cotton balls	_____	_____
• Nail polish remover	_____	_____

- Emery boards   _____   _____
- Cleanser   _____   _____
- Glass cleaner   _____   _____
- Sponge(s)   _____   _____
- Paper towels   _____   _____
- Sample-size toothpaste, mouth-
  wash, shampoo   _____   _____
- Replacement light bulbs   _____   _____

Window shades or curtains for
  privacy   _____   _____

Functional exhaust fan in room or
  window   _____   _____

WHAT IF YOU DON'T HAVE THE RIGHT HOUSE?

Use the material presented in this chapter to evaluate a possible new home. Many people who take my course in New York City live in small apartments and hope that B&B will be a way to help finance a large apartment or a move to a house. Older couples considering a change in life-style after retirement may also anticipate moving. First decide where you would be most happy living. Not everyone enjoys country life. Remember, your guests will visit for short stays, but you will be living there all the time. Examine the seasonal nature of the location, and ask yourself the other location questions that determine how often people will be seeking out your area. Evaluate the house in terms of amenities and number of rooms. Calculate how often you will have to have guests in order to bring in enough money to supplement your income. (Read Chapter 4, "Financial Considerations," before doing this.) How often will you be comfortable having guests in your home? Does this fit with how much business you need to do?

UNHOSTED BED AND BREAKFAST

Sometimes a B&B accommodation is referred to as *unhosted*. This is usually a city apartment or a freestanding cottage or carriage house on the host family's property. In many cities, the demand for reasonably priced apartments for the business traveler on short-term assignment is great, but supply is short. A person who owns or leases an apartment that he or she is not currently using may list it with a reservation service for guest use on a daily or weekly basis. For example, a host may be living with someone but may be reluctant to give up his or her apartment in case the relationship does not last. He or she may be trying to hold onto a small apartment after moving to a larger one because apartment values are rising and selling it next year may mean more money. Using that small apartment for B&B pays the carrying cost and possibly more during the interim. A host may be on vacation or sabbatical for a few weeks or months and allows guests to use the apartment during that time. I know of two young women with small apartments, neither big enough to share with a guest, who take turns sharing with each other, freeing the second apartment for guest use. They split the proceeds.

These are a few of the many types of unhosted places made available for guest use. In many cases, there is a host who makes sure that the apartment is clean and stocked with breakfast food for the guest to prepare. When a host is not in town, he or she must arrange for a friend or concierge service (a company set up to stand in for you for a fee) to be at the apartment to greet guests and acquaint them with any particulars about the place or neighborhood as needed. One of my hosts makes his studio apartment available for guests in New York City and has put together a beautiful book of handy information for his guests. It includes information about restaurants, theater, shopping, as well as laundry facilities and garbage disposal. In all unhosted situations, it is essential that the guest have the phone number of the host or the person in charge in case of emergency.

REAL ESTATE SPECULATION

There are rare people who have an intuitive sense of the real estate market and areas that they believe will rise in value. Such a person can purchase an undervalued home, make improvements to it and use it as a B&B to offset some of the expenses and enjoy the tax benefits while building equity to reap at the time of sale. These people, however, realize that they are gambling. If this type of property is not the owner's primary home, he or she may pay a manager to run the B&B. Making a profit in this situation is unusual, but because the business is planned for a short term only, the losses sustained may be more than made up by the sale of the property.

❖❖❖❖❖❖❖

Question: I have one guest room on the ground floor with a private bath and private entrance. The upstairs guest room shares the family bath. There is a large closet in that room which could be made into a small bathroom. Would it be worthwhile for us to make this additional bathroom?

Answer: My answer to this question is another question: How long have you wanted to do this? If adding this bath is something you have wanted to do for a long time, now is the ideal time. Understand that the difference in what you will be able to charge for this room may only be $10 a night because of the private bath, but you will probably have more call for the room. The cost of the new bath will be a tax deduction, and you will also be increasing your equity in your home. If you decide not to add the bath, you will attract guests who are willing to share the family bath in order to pay lower room cost. Make sure that you are also comfortable sharing your bath with guests. All personal items must be removed from the bath so that guests don't feel that they are invading your personal space.

59

❖❖❖❖❖❖❖

Question: We bought our home a few years ago, and it needed lots of work. Now the public rooms are ready, but all the bedrooms still need to be decorated. Would it be premature to fix up one room and begin while we work on the other two?

Answer: No, most people take it one room at a time. Select your largest room to prepare first. Ideally, a double bed plus a daybed will give you maximum flexibility. You can work on your other bedrooms one by one and open them as they are ready and your business grows.

❖❖❖❖❖❖❖

Question: Please describe a home rejected by your reservation service.

Answer: A potential hostess in Yonkers, New York, arranged for me to visit her two-bedroom, two-bath apartment. The guest room was large, airy, and recently painted light lavender. The bed was covered with stuffed animals. I remarked that with the animals removed and a little decoration, the room would be quite suitable for a business person on short-term assignment or for anyone while looking to relocate in lower Westchester. She smiled and asked, "How many animals will have to go?" All of them, said I, assuming that they belonged to a daughter who was now married or at least away at school. She told me that her daughter is fourteen years old, goes to high school, and lives at home. Her clothes are in the closet and dresser drawers, and she would be very upset if her animals were dispossessed. She explained that the girl falls asleep on the living room couch watching TV every night and no longer sleeps in her own bed. What this woman didn't understand was that she really didn't have a room to rent. No B&B guest at any price wants to feel that he or she is invading anyone's private space.

❖❖❖❖❖❖❖

Question: In looking at my home, I think guests would enjoy my master bedroom most because it has its own bath and a fireplace. The current guest bedroom is next to my daughter's room and shares a bath with her. I think both the guest and my daughter might be uncomfortable with such an arrangement. My daughter is sixteen and will be going to college in two years. Should I give up my master bedroom?

Answer: *The answer to this question depends on a few conditions. First, are you married? If you are, discuss the idea with your spouse. You may decide that relocating is a poor idea after all. You might wait the two years until your daughter leaves for school and then have two guest rooms with a shared bath. However, if you are alone and don't mind changing bedrooms, you are right, this would be an ideal B&B situation. Starting now will certainly help you to accumulate the funds you will need to keep your daughter in college. If she knows that this is your motivation for opening your home to paying guests, you may find her very helpful in keeping the house neat and clean and welcoming the guests.*

❖❖❖❖❖❖❖

Question: Are there state or local regulations that pertain to using my home as a B&B?

Answer: *Chapter 5 goes into considerable depth about these. Please make sure to read it carefully before opening your home or purchasing a place for B&B.*

4

·· **4** ··

Financial Considerations

Bed and Breakfast does not guarantee any homeowner any minimum amount of money per year. It is best to think of this income as money for extras, not money you must have in order to meet basic obligations. Many successful hosts combine their B&B activities with other compatible uses of their homes to generate the money they need if they do not work outside the home. The financial considerations discussed in this chapter include estimating your B&B income, pricing your accommodations, taxes, and record keeping. I also touch briefly on ways to offer additional services to bring in extra income.

ESTIMATING INCOME

How much you might earn from doing Bed and Breakfast is highly variable. Much obviously depends on the types of rooms you offer, how many you have available, how often they are filled (which is sometimes a function of your location), and the price you charge for each overnight stay. Often your reservation service can help you arrive at some good "guesstimates." Remember, there is tremendous variation from season to season and place to place. And be reassured that your second year's estimates will be much more accurate than those for your first.

In a major metropolitan area where room rates in hotels are in the $100-a-night category, a Bed and Breakfast with three or four executive level guest rooms that are occupied 60 per cent of the time, with no restrictions on who is an acceptable guest, and serving good but simple breakfasts might clear $10,000 to $15,000 a year.

A spare room used during only part of the year for guests, in a house in a small college town in the Midwest, where smokers and children are not welcome might have guests on half of the weekends March through October and bring in $1,000 a year.

Remember, the gross income is not the only consideration. B&B is usually most beneficial as a second income. Certainly no one could live in a six-bedroom Victorian home in Croton with a gross income of $15,000 a year. The fact that my husband's income is highly taxed makes the advantages of writing off many of our home expenses another good financial reason to offer Bed & Breakfast in your home.

It is best to make very conservative estimates; after all, it never hurts to find you've surpassed your expectations. Let's first try to estimate how many *roomnights* you can expect in the coming year. A roomnight is the number of rooms multiplied by the number of nights a party stays. If a party of four comes for a two-day stay, they represent two rooms times two nights or four roomnights of business. You may be wondering, "How can I estimate my number of roomnights?" Talk to the reservation service in your area. Find out when the travel season is. Are there tourist attractions near you that will bring people during the travel season? If there are, estimate that you will be three-quarters full on at least half the weekends in the travel season. If you are very selective about who comes (for instance, if you take only nonsmoking couples with no children and no pet allergies), reduce your estimate to two-thirds full.

Following are a few brief examples of how different B&B hosts figured out their likely rates of occupancy.

❖❖❖❖❖❖❖

Becky's B&B is executive quality, about an hour from a major East Coast city, has four rooms that share two baths, is near some tourist attractions, and takes only nonsmokers, but will accept singles and children. A chain hotel room of comparable quality in the area begins at $85. Becky's room rates are $35 for a single, $50 for a double on a daily basis, $200 for a single and $280 for a double on a weekly basis. The travel season in her area is April through October (seven months, twenty-eight weekends). If we estimate three-fourths full for half of those weekends, she will average three rooms of guests two nights per weekend, or six roomnights times fourteen weeks. This would come out to eighty-four roomnights for weekend guests in season. Estimating a 50 percent cutback during off-season, three roomnights times ten weeks (half of the five-month off-season) would give her another thirty roomnights of weekend guests. This leaves four weeks of vacation or time that her house is used for personal friends and not available for B&B guests regardless of demand. Since most weekend guests will be doubles, $50 times 114 roomnights would be $5,700. Becky's place is also near a few major corporations. She can expect either 1 long-term stay (a single executive relocating into the area) of two or three months ($200 a week times ten weeks yields $2,000) or perhaps a few two- or three-week guests on short-term business assignment (auditing a plant, supervising new construction) bringing in five weeks of business times $200, equaling $1,000. Her home is on the way north to a ski area, and some guests will want to stop over on their way to or from their vacation. So add ten roomnights at $50 ($500). In addition, there will be some weekday business from people coming into town to visit relatives who are ill, having a reunion, christening a new baby, attending graduation, or for other personal reasons; add twenty roomnights at $50, or $1,000. A conservative estimate for Becky's B&B would be a gross income of $10,200. Of course, this is not all profit. But Becky can certainly expect that as she becomes better known and gets repeat business and more referrals from satisfied guests, her business will grow and perhaps double in two to three years.

❖❖❖❖❖❖

Susie has a two-bedroom, two-bath New York City apartment in a good location. It is a deluxe accommodation in an area where hotel prices are high. Until now, she has had a roommate who paid $500 a month rent but was always around and had kitchen privileges. There was never anyplace to accommodate Susie's friends or relatives when they came to town. Susie decided that her place would appeal to business people and that she would like to try to have the apartment for personal use on weekends. It is available Monday through Friday. Rates are $60 single, $70 double. If she has paying guests ten days a month, she grosses $600 minimum, or $7,200 a year. If she does more business or has doubles instead of singles on a few of the nights, her income goes up considerably.

❖❖❖❖❖❖

Marsha lives in a rural area a good two hours from the nearest large city. There are no chain hotels nearby, but there is a mom-and-pop motel that charges $40 a night. Although there are no major businesses nearby, she is in a very scenic location with lots of property, hunting, fishing, and pond swimming and skating on her property. There is a college twenty minutes away, and the exit to the main highway connecting two major cities in the state is only five minutes away. She has three rooms available for guests; they share a guest bath. One daughter still lives at home, and there is an extra bed in the daughter's room for a visiting child. Marsha can expect to have guests on the four weekends that the college has home football games, parents' weekend, and graduation and also to have an occasional parent coming up overnight with their son or daughter to visit the college for a personal interview. Estimate thirty-eight room-nights of college-related guests at $35 per night, or $1,330. If Marsha markets her B&B properly, city folk might make the trip to enjoy three-day weekends in this nature lover's paradise. Add another thirty-six roomnights, or $1,260. Residents of the town will also call on Marsha to accommodate guests for weddings, family reunions and the like. Add twenty-five roomnights, or $875. Marsha can expect to gross $3,165.

❖❖❖❖❖❖❖

Diana has a fabulous place—a bedroom with fireplace, king-sized bed, mountain views, private bath, and Jacuzzi. She likes to feature gourmet breakfasts or breakfast in bed. She and her husband love to entertain and have a VCR and a large collection of old movies on tape. The location is close to a number of colleges, tourist attractions, and businesses in southern California. The problem Diana faces is that the area is overbuilt, with hotels that offer rooms with breakfast for $29.95. Diana's house is worth over $500,000. It is not worth her time to try to compete with a cheap motel by offering a lower price. She realizes that what she offers is a fantasy, a romantic getaway. She charges $75 a night for a couple and for $125 will include a candlelight supper. She expects her guests to come only from a certain segment of the travel market, exactly the type she wants to entertain, people who will be much like her husband and herself, with similar interests. She limits her business to two weekends a month and expects to earn $4,600 (about $200 per weekend, twenty-three weekends a year).

❖❖❖❖❖❖❖

Donald is a mystery writer who has restored a six-bedroom home in the French Quarter of New Orleans. Each room now has a private bath. Two of the bedrooms open into a sitting room suite. Two ground-floor bedrooms open onto private gardens at the rear. Donald's rates are $150 a night for the two-bedroom suite, $75 each for his garden rooms, and $65 for a room with a queen-sized bed. Donald's decor is deluxe, and the location is very desirable for business travelers, conventioneers, and tourists. He is fully booked about five days a week, which brings in $365 per day, $1,825 per week. Donald enjoys traveling and finds that the summer is his off-season, so that's when he closes up and goes off on his own. Open forty weeks a year, Donald grosses $73,000 from his B&B.

❖❖❖❖❖❖❖

Sue Ellen and her husband and three youngsters (ages five, seven, and nine) live in a rural area in Wisconsin. They have a dairy farm and have fixed up the farmhand's cottage to sleep a family of four. Guests who come there are welcome to take all meals with the family because there are few restaurants within a twenty-mile radius. (Meals other than breakfast are extra.) Guests can relax or pitch in with farm chores. Children are welcome to learn to milk a cow, meet the newborn calf, gather eggs from the chickens, or play inside by the wood-burning stove on cold rainy days. Sue Ellen keeps lots of games handy for such days. Guests can go for a moonlit ride on the hay wagon in the summer and snowmobiling in the winter. The hunting season in the fall draws hunters from as far away as Chicago. Rates here are $30 for two people, $10 each for children over three years old or adults sharing the cottage. Her first year, Sue Ellen got a lot of hunters during the brief hunting season ($500). Winter (November through March) offered lots to do, but there was so much snow that a number of guests canceled their reservations because they couldn't get there. She only grossed $1,000. In summer, families of four came about four days a month ($400). In total, Sue Ellen earned about $2,000; she could probably have rented her cottage full time and earned about the same thing. Instead, she enjoyed the variety of guests and found that her children benefited from the interactions with other children from less rural surroundings.

67

PRICING

In the preceding examples, the information given included how much each room cost. Understand that location is one of the key ingredients; B&B rates vary across the country and around the world for some of the same reasons that the cost of housing (supply and demand) varies. It is usually more expensive to stay in the city than the country. The other factor in determining price is amenities. A deluxe accommodation will charge more than a standard or executive one in the same location.

In the beginning of B&B in this country, the media focused on the "sleep cheap" aspect. As more high-quality accommodations became available, guests who called to get reservations were stunned to find that prices were far more than $15 a night. It is important for guests to realize that whatever a B&B charges, it should be a real value compared with an equivalent commercial accommodation. For example, if a chain hotel's rooms in your area cost $85 and do not include breakfast, an executive-quality home should probably charge no more than $50 to $60 with breakfast. B&B's generally average half to two-thirds the cost of a comparable-class hotel or motel. Certainly, there are going to be cheaper places to stay in the area, but they won't be as nice as yours, and you should not try to compete with them on price. Guests looking only for a low price aren't usually going to be the ones B&B hosts seek, anyway.

Your reservation service will be the best place to turn to for help in pricing. The staff knows what comparable places go for and can sometimes give you pricing ideas that will make your place very attractive to potential guests. You can always adjust your rates in the future, but it is good to set a price that you can live with for at least a year because it would be awkward for anyone representing you to print prices, send them out to guests, and then have to say that the printed prices are wrong.

In thinking of pricing, decide if you want to give a discount for children, weekly stays, or senior citizens.

There is customarily no charge for children under two staying in the same room with parents. For children over three and under twelve, the rate is generally $10. If the children stay in a separate room, you have the option of charging a child rate or an adult rate. Logically, if they take up another room, they should be charged for it. Unfortunately, many B&B's don't have space or extra beds to accommodate children with their parents, and the charge for two rooms can be more than a family wants to pay. For this reason B&B's don't get very many families as guests.

Weekly prices may be the equivalent of six nights' stay, five nights' stay, or $10 off per night. The lower rate is charged because usually weekly stays are much easier on the hostess (not a lot of bed changing) and guests staying for a long time don't usually expect a gourmet breakfast every day. Because so much of the business is on weekends, weekly rates encourage people who will be in town during the week to use a B&B. Increasing your number of roomnights results in increasing your business. A $50-a-night room that is empty brings you in $0. But if you reduce your nightly rate to $40 to bring in a week's stay, you will make $280.

Guests sometimes think that they can book a room for Saturday night, arrive Saturday at 10:00 A.M., and hang around until late Sunday afternoon, really enjoying a full weekend at the cost of a one-night accommodation. This is the reason that hosts in desirable locations have two-night minimum stays on weekends and even three nights on long weekends. This is particularly true in places with very short seasons, such as beach and ski areas. Decide if you want to set a minimum length of stay. If you have a two-night minimum and are free on a Saturday night, you can always call your service to say that you will be willing to accept a last-minute one-night guest.

EXPENSES

There are definitely expenses related to operating a Bed and Breakfast. At the very least, you will be sprucing up; freshening paint; investing in new sheets, towels, and table linens; and purchasing a guest book. You may want to invest in new furniture or antiques, landscaping, a pool, and who knows what else. You may have structural repairs to make or restoration to do. The important thing to understand is that because these expenses are now related to business use, not just personal use, you must keep receipts and understand how they will be reflected in your tax obligations.

INCOME TAX

Examine the tax position of your non-B&B income. With a B&B, portions of your mortgage payment, house maintenance expenses, and utilities are deductible from your taxable income. For many hosts, this tax savings is a far more important financial reason for getting into the business than the actual dollars paid by guests. Although you don't have the fun of receiving the cash in your hand, the bottom line of your tax return may look tremendously different because of your B&B especially if your living expenses are sizable.

You will be able to claim these expenses only if you itemize your deductions, so you will want to keep accurate records of them. Most will fall into one of five categories: guest capital expenses, guest maintenance expenses, house capital expenses, house maintenance expenses, and business expenses.

Guest Capital Expenses. These are expenses for things that you purchase exclusively for guest use that will last longer than a year. For example, an antique bedroom set with bed, marble-topped dresser, and armoire: $1,000. Other guest capital expenses might include:

- TV for guest room

- Blankets or quilts

- Breakfast trays

- Plants for guest room

- Furniture for guest room

- Draperies or window shades for guest room

- Guest room carpeting

- Artwork for guest room

- Towel rack

- Smoke detectors and fire extinguishers

Guest Maintenance Expenses. These are expenses for things bought exclusively for the guests use that will last less than a year. For example, flowers for the guest room: $2.50. Other guest maintenance expenses might include:

- Fruit placed in guest room

- Newspapers in guest room

- Magazines for guest bathroom

- Repairs to guest furniture

- Sheets, towels, and table linens

- Breakfast-related costs

House Capital Expenses. Thcsc are expenses for things for the house that will be used in common by your family and the guests and that will last more than a year. For example, a new room: $4,000. Other house capital expenditures may include:

- Furniture for public rooms

- A new kitchen or appliances

- TV in the family room

- Hot tub, Jacuzzi, pool, tennis courts

- Carpeting

- Outdoor landscaping

House Maintenance Expenses. These are expenses for things for the house that will be used in common by your family and the guests but that will last less than a year. For example, the gardner's services. Other house maintenance expenses may include:

- Heat

- Electricity and gas

- Telephone

- Rent

- Housekeeper or laundress

- Painter

- Handyman

- Plumber

- Heavy cleaning service

- Pool service

- Interior designer

Business Expenses. These are expenses incurred in order to do business. For example, your accountant's fees. Other business expenses may include:

- Your attorney's fees

- Your ledger

- Business cards or stationery

- Liability insurance

- Membership in a reservation service, chamber of commerce, other professional group

- Telephone answering machine

- Reservation service commissions

- Advertising

- Baby-sitter's fees while you take guests on tours of your area

What will not fit into these five categories are items bought for the exclusive personal use of you and your family and are not deductible. It is wise to sit down with your accountant and discuss the tax implications and benefits. I am not an accountant, but it is my understanding that you can deduct your total guest maintenance expenses, your business expenses, and a portion of your home maintenance costs in the tax year in which these expenses are incurred. Your guest capital expenses will be fully deductible but depreciated over time according to the IRS ruling on the life of each type of expense. For example, furniture is depreciated over ten years; so the $1,000 antique bedroom set would be depreciated at $100 a year over ten years.

House capital expenses are also depreciated. But because you use the house in common with the guests, only a portion of these expenses will be allowed. It is necessary to determine the amount of your home used for business and the proportion of the year during which it is used for business.

For example, in Donna's four-bedroom home, two bedrooms are used exclusively for B&B. The first floor of the home includes the kitchen, where breakfast is prepared; the living room, where guests sit in front of the fire and relax; the dining room, where breakfast is served; and the family room, where guests watch television. Half of the second floor (where the bedrooms are) is used exclusively by guests. The first floor is used in common by the family and guests. Thus, half of the home is used for business.

If the family has guests in any week, the house must be heated or cooled, cleaned, have electricity, telephone, service, and so on. These things are not turned on and off daily, so it seems appropriate to count weeks that a B&B does business. If there were guests overnight during ten or more weeks, it is fair to say that the B&B did business one-quarter of the year. If guests came in more than twenty weeks, the B&B did business half of the year. More than forty weeks represents full-time use because every business is entitled to some vacation and time when the business is open but makes no sales.

Since Donna uses half of her house, if she is in business one-quarter of the year, it would be fair for her to use one-eighth (one-half times one-fourth) of all house maintenance and house capital expenditures as deductions. If her business grows and she builds it into a full-time business (half of the house times one year), it would be appropriate for her to deduct half of all house expenses. This same figure applies to the amount of house maintenance expenses in the year incurred and the portion of house capital expenditures written off over time.

To keep track of my expenses and to make it easier for my accountant, I have always kept five large envelopes to which I have attached ledger paper. On each envelope, I write the type of expense (e.g., guest capital expenses) and the tax year. I look at each receipt, ask myself which category the expense falls under, write the amount and what was bought on the ledger paper, and drop the receipt into the envelope. This way, I have made a record of the expense while it is still fresh in my mind, and the backup is in the envelope in case of an audit.

BREAKFAST COSTS

Because most hosts don't want to have to group the food they buy for guests separately when they are on line at the supermarket, they find it easier to just keep an accurate count of how many breakfasts are served (the number of guests times the nights they stayed). This cost is then arrived at by multiplying $3.00 for a continental breakfast or $3.50 for a full breakfast. If you serve a very elaborate breakfast—for example, with caviar or fresh maple syrup—the cost may go up to $4.00. Breakfast costs should include more than just the price paid for food. It also includes the cost of gas used driving to and from the market, refrigerating the food until it is used, waste and spoilage, gas or electricity to cook the food, washing the dishes in your dishwasher, and washing table linens in the washing machine. If you purchase fancy centerpieces, fine china, or silver, these costs are included as maintenance or capital expenses.

STAFF

Independent Contractors and Salaried Employees

As long as people who work for you file a self-employment tax return and send you a bill for services rendered or work for you under terms of an independent contractor agreement, you are not responsible for any payroll expenses such as social security or federal or state withholding tax. But if you pay them more than a certain amount, you may be required to file Form 1099 with the IRS. Check with the IRS or your accountant to see what this amount is.

If you hire a full-time housekeeper, for example, you will need to speak to your accountant about setting up a payroll ledger and withholding social security, unemployment insurance, and disability. This procedure is a nuisance, but absolutely essential if you are to claim these expenses.

75

Hiring and Supervising Staff

If you are already established in an area, you may have an accountant and an attorney. If you are new to an area, you will be selecting these professionals as well as a realtor, insurance agent, gardner, plumber, electrician, and so on. The best way to choose from the vast array of vendors offering these services is to speak first to your neighbors and your reservation service. Your neighbors will certainly have had experience with local people and can steer you toward some and away from others. If you have a number of good recommendations, interview them and make your selection based on whether or not you will feel comfortable working with them, they have appropriate credentials, are liked in the community, and have time to give to your business. When I decided that I needed a bookkeeper, I first interviewed the three women who answered my newspaper ad and then had my accountant talk to them. He felt that two were equally qualified, so I hired the one who offered me flexible hours and a reasonable wage.

If you are unhappy with the work that someone is doing for you, speak to them immediately. Make clear exactly what the problem is. This will put them on alert. For example, my gardener didn't seem to show up for work on any particular schedule and sometimes appeared early Saturday morning with two helpers, all making a huge racket with their power mowers, and waking my guests. We discussed it, and he promised to come on weekdays only, when I have very few guests who expect to sleep late in the morning.

If you hire household help, it is often necessary to make a schedule for them so that they will know what your priorities are. The same holds true for such workers as painters and carpenters. You are the client, and those who work for you are the employees. You need to monitor the work done and give people feedback. If you have been satisfied, tell them or write a letter of thanks for a job well done. You will be remembered as appreciative; and if you need another job done in the future, you will have established a positive bond. If you are not satisfied and talking to the person responsible doesn't help, you may need to find someone new to do the work. It is often hard to fire someone, but it is necessary if you don't want your warm nature to be taken advantage of.

Hiring Your Children

Don't forget that under the 1987 tax law, children over fourteen can earn money that will be taxed at their own rate, not yours. If you use them to help care for the house, yard, and guests and pay them for these chores, this part of your profits will be taxed at a low rate and can help to build their college fund. Also, many host families find that running a B&B unites the family in a common purpose, and it is an excellent way to introduce children to the world of work and responsibility.

EXPENSES OFFSET YOUR TAXABLE PROFIT

You will pay taxes only on that part of your B&B income that exceeds your expenses. As in any new business, start-up costs in the first few years, in combination with low initial volume, may result in losses, which of course are paid for from your other income. In certain respects, this does shelter other income. However, you cannot continue to show a loss year after year. In five years, two years must show a profit. After that, if you make a major investment in your home (e.g., to remodel, restore, or add a pool) to increase its desirability as a B&B, you will again be able to justify a period of loss.

The important thing is that you must be able to prove your B&B is a serious business, not a hobby. The IRS considers hobby income to be very different from that of a small business. Although all the income from a hobby is taxable, expenses related to carrying it out are not. For example, if you decided to keep bees for a hobby and incidentally sold a few jars of the honey to your friends and neighbors, the money paid you would be taxable, but the cost of the jars and lids would not be deductible.

DEPRECIATING YOUR HOME

One of the most complicated issues most hosts face is whether or not to depreciate that portion of the home used as a business. Although it may be wise for an older person in a very high tax bracket who has lived only a short time in a very expensive house to depreciate as much of it as is allowed, it may be unwise for someone who is younger, intends to move in a few years, or bought the house a long time ago to depreciate it. Only you and your accountant can figure out what is best for your particular circumstances. The important thing to remember is that if you depreciate a portion of your house now, when you sell it, only the portion that has not been depreciated will count as the expense subtracted from your selling price when computing capital gains. What this means to you varies according to tax bracket as well as age. Some people qualify for a one-time credit on the sale of their primary residence that exempts some of the profit from tax. Others intend to spend the rest of their lives in their home and don't care if their children inherit a house that has been partially depreciated.

❖❖❖❖❖❖❖

Question: Is it permissible to include information about other services I can provide for an extra fee to interested guests? I have a small crafts business and can also arrange special-interest tours to wineries and the studios of other artists in my area.

Answer: By all means, list these interests and capabilities with your reservation service, and make it clear that an addi-

tional fee is charged. Ask your service to place a feature on what you do in your network newsletter so that other hosts can tell their guests, too. Include a descriptive flier or brochure among the materials on tourist attractions in your guest rooms. Here are some examples of supplemental services some hosts offer.

- *Real estate sales or brokering*
- *Breakfast in bed (with the works, popular for honeymooners)*
- *Shopping tours (especially to outlets and fashion discounters)*
- *Picnic lunches or fireside suppers for two*
- *Running local errands at an hourly rate*
- *Interpreting & translating*
- *Crafts and collectibles (for sale in the B&B to guests only)*
- *Antiques for sale*
- *Lessons (sports, needlework, languages, typing)*
- *Office services*
- *Child care*
- *Horse boarding and grooming*
- *Cosmetics or wardrobe consultation*
- *A walking tour of the area*

If you offer a tour that must use a car, please go in the guests' car. If you use your car, you will need a chauffer's license and livery insurance. Remember that it is fine to have literature in the guest room that will let the interested guest know how to avail themselves of your extra services, but don't push. You don't want guests to feel uncomfortable if they aren't interested.

5

$\diamond$ **5** $\diamond$

Starting Up

Most newcomers to Bed and Breakfast needn't reinvent the wheel when starting up. With the experience of 20,000 host families behind them, most reservation services are well versed in assisting new hosts in complying with regulations in their area. Using your reservation service as a resource during your start-up phase will be a great time-saver.

REGULATIONS VARY FROM STATE TO STATE

Because the status of Bed and Breakfast varies from state to state and community to community, based both on written laws and codes and on local custom, it is impossible to provide a specific set of steps to follow to ensure that your B&B will open without a hitch. It is possible, however, to outline the areas of concern every new host must deal with before greeting the first guest.

This chapter presumes that you have established a working relationship with a knowledgeable and responsible reservation service. If there is no service in your immediate area, find the closest by checking the Reservation Service Directory in the Appendix, and call them before you call anyone else. Follow their suggestions for dealing with any agencies or officials. They've been through this many times before, and they want you to open as much as you do. If there is no reservation service covering your area, consider starting one to extend the benefits of B&B to many more people. In fairly short order, you can become the expert advising newcomers.

DETERMINING YOUR NEED FOR A PERMIT

Whereas most commercial places are required to have a license or permit to operate, a private-home B&B may or may not, depending on its location and size. Here are two examples.

New York State looks at it this way: If the occupancy of your home (including your family) averages, on a daily basis, fewer than ten persons, no license or permit is required, and your business is categorized as a private-home B&B. New York also exempts B&B's from the state restaurant code, but does require that all meat served be bought in a store to ensure that it has been inspected by the U.S. Department of Agriculture. It also requires that your water and septic systems be adequate for the needs of your business and that hosts collect sales tax on all stays.

In Wyoming, the Department of Health and Social Services, sees the matter very differently. It regulates B&B's and what it terms *ranch recreation facilities* stringently by requiring that any person operating such a facility shall possess a current, valid permit from the Division of Health and Medical Services. A Bed and Breakfast is defined as any private home that is used to provide accommodation for a charge to the public and that has not more than four lodging units or is occupied by no more than a daily average of eight people during any thirty-day period and in which no more than two family-style meals are provided in any twenty-four-hour period. Clearly, this rule could include B&B inns as well as older-style tourist homes. No distinction is made between walk-in clientele and screened guests. Wyoming reserves the right for the state health officer to make an inspection of any B&B during normal operating hours to ascertain compliance with health and safety conditions. Furthermore, the Wyoming rules specify in detail the types of food one may serve to B&B guests and where food must be prepared (on the premises). The guest may not be offered a choice from a menu. The code also specifies the minimum allowable size of escape windows, the location of mandated smoke detectors, a written record of monthly checks of the smoke detectors, and the type of fire extinguishers to be available in good working order.

Your state may lean toward the New York approach or to the Wyoming approach. Because B&B is evolving very rapidly in North America, it is important for you to stay informed, through your reservation service and area networks, of new developments that may affect the conduct of your business.

KEEPING UP TO DATE

The need to provide legislators with background on B&B was one of the main reasons for the formation of Bed & Breakfast Reservation Services Worldwide—A Trade Association, in 1985. Ultimately, though, the responsibility for being in compliance with whatever your state requires falls to you because you are the individual actually providing the service. Attend get-togethers sponsored by your reservation service, and read your business newsletters to stay up-to-date.

By the way, if your business is larger than your state's definition of a B&B, you will probably have to comply with all the provisions of the state's commercial code, just like any inn, hotel, or motel, even if you accept only screened guests through your reservation service. It is important to know from the very start what scale of business you want to get into. The regulations and the cost of conforming to them may help you to decide.

Make it a point to attend seminars and workshops for small-business operators that may be offered free of charge by your community college or local bank. (Many are organized specifically for women starting new businesses.)

FIRE AND SAFETY CODES

In January 1984, New York State passed the most stringent fire and safety code in the country. It was in response to a terrible hotel fire the year before. When an investigation found that the hotel had not been in violation of the existing code, the legislature decided that something was wrong with the code. The new code applies to any place that opens after January, 1984 and takes more than four guests on a routine basis. The implications are that private-home B&B's with more than three guest rooms have to conform to the new code. This is very expensive, involving sprinkler systems, self-closing fire doors on each guest room, extra stairs or full fire escapes, and more. I include this information because often one state will follow another in developing statutes and New York has often been such a leader. Before you open your door to guests, check your state's fire and safety code provisions. If your house is on a historic register, you can sometimes secure an exemption from various requirements, but you can't ignore requirements just because you have a historic home.

SALES TAX

In most states, you will be required to charge guests sales tax. Your reservation service may or may not handle this for you. It will always inform a guest that this tax is due and to whom it is to be paid. But remember, your reservation service does not maintain your business records; you do. The easiest way for you to keep track of all your B&B business matters is by entering expenses and income into a common ledger. Some hosts now use a computer spreadsheet designed for the small-business operator, but this level of record keeping is probably not necessary or helpful unless you have several rooms and do a considerable amount of business.

The reservation service typically receives the required deposit on a reservation and forwards the entire sum, less its commission (usually 20 to 30 percent), to you. You should enter the entire sum to be paid by the guests under income and the reservation service commission as an expense of doing business.

Sales tax is payable on the total nightly cost for your room(s). You compute the tax applicable in your area based on tables supplied by your state and collect it in addition to any balance due from your guests. The sales tax is not entered as income to you because you are merely acting as an agent in collecting it. Because it is not income, it is not deductible on your tax return. It is a good idea to talk to your accountant about your tax responsibilities and how to take care of them with the least amount of effort.

Generally, sales tax is reported and remitted to the state every quarter. Failure to collect or remit sales tax may be punishable by a fine in many states. In New York State, a law was passed in 1985 requiring that sales tax forms be filed even for a quarter in which you had no income and collected no tax. Failure to file costs you a $50 fine. Filing late can cost you interest on tax money due the state, so take the few minutes that are necessary each quarter to fill out and send in your tax forms and money on time. Keep current at the end of each month and quarterly filing will be a breeze.

RECORD KEEPING

Most hosts will not need a bookkeeper. The records you maintain to monitor your business and pay sales tax and income tax should be perfectly adequate. For sales tax, use the remittance schedule and forms supplied by the state. Federal income tax requires that you file a Schedule C with your annual return, itemizing your business expenses and deductions. State and city income taxes are usually based on your adjusted federal income.

Your Guest Book

You will need to keep a guest book for your guests to sign when they arrive. It can be simple, perhaps nothing more than a composition notebook, or fancy. There should be space for the guest's name, home address, telephone number, and comments. Some hosts place photographs of guests in the book, cover the book with decorative fabric, and send copies of the photos in holiday cards. This serves to increase repeat and word-of-mouth business. Moreover, this type of register can help you to keep names and faces together long after guests have departed. You may even want to jot down something next to the guest's name (for instance, "came for son's graduation") so that you will be reminded when you communicate with this guest in the future. In addition, it provides a legal account of your guests in the rare event that there should be an audit of your business or an inquiry by local planning, zoning, or other officials.

I also keep a lined piece of paper for each month with the following entries:

Name	Nights	Dates	Number in Party	Total Paid	Commission	Tax
Mary Smith	2	9/15–9/17	2	$80	$16	$4.60

At the end of each month, I total up the columns and compute the number of breakfasts served. I then know gross sales, commissions paid out, breakfast costs, and sales tax owed. I always keep the sales tax money separate from money that belongs to me so that when it comes time to pay, it won't feel like my money. Your ledger and guest book are generally all you need to manage your sales tax records. They are all you would ever be asked to produce to document that the sales tax you have paid for any given period of time is correct.

Income Tax

For federal income taxes, a much more detailed and comprehensive set of records and receipts needs to be kept. Your accountant can help you set up a system for storing and organizing all documents for tax time, or you may wish to utilize my large-envelope method (see Chapter 4).

A number of firms now offer a *one-write system*: Each time you write a check, it is spread into columns for the various types of expenditures you have. At the end of each month, simply add up the columns to keep a current account of expenses. The same type of system can be used to record incoming funds and their sources. Keeping good records helps your accountant a great deal at tax time. It also gives you a very good idea of how your business is doing. You still need to keep actual receipts for expenditures (to produce in case of a tax audit to document that the checks you wrote did, indeed, go for payment of bills you claim), but this form of business checkbook tells you exactly where you stand whenever you want to know.

ZONING

Zoning is always a local issue. My experience with zoning will give you an idea of the worst-possible scenario, one that resulted in part because I was the first B&B in my area. It is unlikely that you will experience something similar, but what I learned should help you to anticipate any obstacles with local zoning that might affect you.

Before starting my business, I had checked with state agencies controlling licenses and permits and with the health department and gotten the okay to proceed as long as we had fewer than ten persons staying in our home on an average night. (New York State considers ten people on a daily basis the definition of a temporary residence, the smallest commercial entity of this type.) I thought I had covered all bases. It never dawned on me that sleeping and eating were not consistent with residential use. One of my neighbors, however, had other ideas. She could not have been more upset if we had opened a brothel. She went about the neighborhood gathering support to stamp out "the B&B menace."

Once we appeared on the front page of the local paper in a story about the reservation service; she complained to the zoning officials that we were operating a commercial business in a residential neighborhood and demanded that something be done immediately. The zoning official rang my bell and proceeded to let me know that, in Croton, only one boarder is permitted in residential neighborhoods. Therefore, if we had one couple or one family as guests, we were in violation of the zoning code. I replied that these were not boarders but guests, about whom the code said nothing. He suggested that we go before the zoning board to get their opinion. Having never been to a zoning meeting, but being a rational person (however politically inexperienced), I agreed. I was in for a rude awakening. To start, the board sends out letters to every neighbor within four hundred feet of a home to be discussed to let them know about the meeting.

Meanwhile, my adversary continued to gather support for her cause. Her fears were as follows: If Bed and Breakfasts were allowed in residential neighborhoods, soon there would be B&B's all over town. Strangers would be riding around town looking for them. Large tractor trailer trucks would be parked in the streets. Couples would be dropping by, by the hour. Property values would surely plummet. She convinced one gentleman down the road to write a letter to the local paper saying. "People will be ringing our doorbell at 3:00 A.M. looking for the mini-motel."

The night of the zoning meeting arrived. Clusters of people were seated all around the room. In one corner was the opposition to the local day-care project. In another were the neighbors who didn't want a family to increase the size of its driveway. Prominently seated were my neighbor and her supporters. In support of Bed and Breakfast were myself and my husband, one set of our immediate neighbors, and another couple from down the block.

I spoke. My view was that a boarder is, by definition, a resident of the community. When asked his or her address, a boarder gives your address. A boarder can get a library card, send his or her child to the local school, and in general enjoys all rights and privileges of any other resident, including voting. B&B guests, by contrast, are under no delusion that my home is theirs. They have a home somewhere else, where they vote, pay taxes, and use the city services. Bed and Breakfast guests are merely visitors who come with travel dollars in their pockets to shop in our shops and eat in our restaurants, stimulating the local economy and taking home with them a pleasant memory about our town.

After I spoke, a number of other people stood up to have their say. They went on as though I had said that a B&B guest *was* really a boarder and should be allowed as such. The other citizens present clearly believed that a B&B guest was not a boarder. Indeed, the zoning board reached the conclusion that, although they didn't know what a B&B guest was, it certainly wasn't a boarder. I was amazed that in this public forum most of the speakers were content to give opinions based on emotion rather than fact. Many of those who spoke had not come for this issue in the first place and were totally uninformed about how our B&B worked. They didn't know that the reservation service did all the promotion and that we were not open to the public, only to those with reservations.

The zoning board seemed to be measuring the climate of

the room. Was this group warm or cold to the issue at hand? They acted as though this small group of people truly represented the sentiments of the village at large, which couldn't have been farther from the truth. Once the issue was getting front-page coverage in the local papers, strangers would come up to me in the supermarket to say what a lovely idea it was to have a B&B in town. But these people were not at the zoning hearing meeting. No doubt it never occurred to them that something so sensible would have any trouble being approved. The upshot of our appearance before the board was that because they had said B&B guests were not boarders, we felt it was perfectly legal to continue our business.

The board, however, thought that the ruling meant B&B's were not allowed, although they had not said this as such. In New York State and most others, anything that is not expressly prohibited in local zoning is permitted, so we continued to take guests. Again our doorbell rang. This time the zoning official said it was his duty to tell us to cease and desist this activity, or the village would issue a subpoena to take us to court. I knew it was time to talk to a lawyer.

I called a local attorney who had been instrumental in writing the zoning code. In his opinion, our B&B was a "customary home occupation." This is a category included in most zoning codes but that varies slightly in definition from locale to locale. Our code restricted a customary home occupation to one-third of the square footage of the house, forbade any sign outside, and permitted no employees. We agreed that we met those criteria, and our lawyer assured us that this would probably be the end of our problems because the village doesn't generally take residents to court. Famous last words! A few days later, a summons arrived charging me with flagrantly and knowingly violating the zoning code and ordering me to appear in criminal court. Panic! I envisioned myself in jail. Vertical stripes do nothing for my appearance. After some serious discussion with my husband, we agreed to spend up to our entire earnings to date ($1,500) for defense. I called the lawyer and told him to start his meter running.

I also decided that to justify the expense of the trial, I would do everything I could to make sure that publicity about it would appear on major television stations and in *The New York Times*. This was definitely the riskiest thing I had ever done. I knew that if we lost in court, we would have to fold our tent. But if we won, what a wonderful way to let the world know about B&B in America!

The day of our court appearance drew near. A large story about the controversy appeared in the real estate section of the Sunday *New York Times*. A national network did a five-minute spot on the 6:00 P.M. news. The day of the trial, a local television reporter sat in the courtroom with her camera crew, ready to interview the judge on the courtroom steps.

Our witnesses were ready. An author of a best-selling B&B book and officer of the American Bed & Breakfast Association, testified that Bed and Breakfast was going on in 5,000 homes across America, 98 percent of which were in residentially zoned homes. A representative of the New York State Department of Commerce, Tourism Division, testified that the state encouraged the development of B&B because it would be especially helpful to small communities where demand for accommodations was too small or too seasonal to support commercial facilities. I testified as to how our reservation service worked to screen guests and send them by advance reservation to the homes listed with our group.

The best part of going to court was that the issue was truly whether we were violating a law. The neighbors were not in court. Witnesses were asked to state facts, not give opinions; and the judge looked at the law and the evidence, weighed both, and acquitted us. This case, although at the village level, has been a precedent-setting one in the state.

Today, more than four years later, none of our neighbor's fears have been realized. There are only two B&B's in Croton, and there have been no negative incidents related to them. Property values around our homes have never been higher. The village has referred a number of guests to the reservation service. And the judge even asked us if we would host a wedding at which there would be no guests and we would have to stand up for the bride and groom. The wedding took place on a beautiful spring day, the one weekend of the year when my weeping Chinese cherry was in full bloom, with pink blossoms from top to bottom. My daughter got to be the flower girl. In all, a very good omen for things to come.

YOU BENEFIT FROM MY ORDEAL

Most hosts won't have to fight such a battle themselves. It is important to read your town's zoning code manual. It is best not to walk into your town hall and say, "I want to open a B&B." If you're the first one, you will most likely be told that it's not permitted even if they don't really know. They can confuse what you plan to do with a tourist home, which needs to be in the commercially zoned area. If you take guests only by reservation and have no sign outside, you can probably fit under the customary home occupation category and be legal in a residential zone. So just go into the town hall, purchase a copy of the zoning code, and read it carefully at your own pace. Look under "Bed and Breakfast," which you probably won't find. Then look under "Customary Home Occupation" and see if the requirements are compatible with what you plan to do. Realize that if you plan to have more than three or four guest rooms, your business may be too large to be considered a noncommercial use of your home. If you have any uncertainty, speak to a local zoning lawyer.

If it becomes necessary to get a variance from your zoning board, have your attorney represent you, and make sure to have as many local people as possible present to support you. If the code seems compatible with what you plan, don't go before a zoning board unnecessarily. If your town passes a law pertaining to Bed and Breakfast after you are in operation, it cannot legislate you out of business. Your business would be considered a nonconforming but preexisting use. My town, after losing in court, developed a special permit required for any new B&B's. But it does not apply to me, since I am covered by a grandfather clause. New B&B's in Croton must now be inspected by the village inspector, must comply with current fire and safety requirements, must have adequate off-street parking, and must pay an annual fee to the village to renew the permit.

As Bed and Breakfast becomes more common, it should be less difficult for homeowners to work with local government. It is certainly an asset, especially in a small community, to have this type of accommodation readily available.

Where there have been serious problems for hosts (Carmel, California, and Sante Fe, New Mexico), the outcry has come from hotels and motels which are overbuilt and fear that every empty room represents a guest stolen from them by a B&B. The mayor of Sante Fe recently made a speech saying how proud he was to have stopped the spread of B&B in his city. The industry has been forced to go underground there. America has always been a place that afforded freedom to all citizens. And I believe people should have the right to choose a cozy B&B environment over a cold, impersonal hotel room. Legislators must be made to see this point of view and to realize that those travelers who want to sample a bit of regional life will go to other towns that do have B&B's. Surely it is in the best interest of towns all over America to offer this choice to travelers.

SLEEPING ARRANGEMENTS

It's always necessary to ask your guests what sleeping arrangements are needed. Problems develop when hosts make assumptions. Often a married couple may require twin beds because this is the only way that they are comfortable sleeping. In today's culture, we also see a lot of unmarried couples travelling together. If you have a problem with unmarried couples sleeping together in your home, you should include this in your literature and inform the reservation service about it. Because your home is your castle, you are free to have only those guests with whom you are comfortable.

The following story illustrates an awkward situation that occurred before I routinely began asking about sleeping arrangements. As you will see, the story also demonstrates the need for checking on your insurance coverage.

In our second year of business, two women booked a room for the weekend. They came by train from New York City, and I put them in the twin-bedded room, which is what I assumed they would prefer. It became apparent to me as they gazed across the hall at the double-bedded room that they were gay. I had made a mistake, but was too embarrassed to offer them the other room. Since this occurrence, I routinely ask about bed preference when booking reservations.

Still, the day progressed nicely. We all swam and played volleyball in the pool and chatted. The women had wonderful senses of humor, and we really got to know and like these bright, articulate, and fun-loving people. Because they had no car and cabs in the country are expensive, we decided to invite them to join us for a barbeque dinner. Gloria (not her real name), a tall movie actress who reminded us of Katherine Hepburn in her youth, went off to the market with George to pick up a steak, while Suzie, a lead singer from a European rock band, came down to the garden with me to pick salad vegetables. She paused by my berry patch and asked me to identify a bright purple berry on a bush with large green leaves. It resembled nothing that I had ever seen in a store, and I told her so. She agreed, but before I could warn her about eating unknown berries, she popped one in her mouth, made a face, and said, "I don't think they are for eating."

We had a wonderful dinner and played some word games; and after a full day of sunshine, swimming, and fresh air, everyone retired early.

At 2:00 A.M. George and I were awakened by a knock on our bedroom door. There was Gloria, who said, "Suzie is lying on the floor of the bathroom, white as a ghost, having just thrown up everything she has eaten in days. It must be *the berry!*" In my mind, I saw large headlines: "Evil Bed and Breakfast Queen Poisons Guest!" Quickly, I pushed George out of bed, ran to the phone to call Poison Control, and told George to take Suzie to the hospital. Poison Control was very helpful; they agreed that the best course of action was indeed to rush her to the hospital and to bring the berry bush with us. So in my nightgown, barefoot, flashlight and ax in hand, I rushed out into the garden to cut it down. George and Gloria carried Suzie to the car, and they sped away. I remained at home with my sleeping toddler and my mother-in-law, who was visiting from California.

At 4:00 A.M., George and Gloria returned, but without Suzie. I was sure she was dead. She was not. The hospital had given her some fluid to counteract the dehydration and an injection to stop the vomiting, and she had fallen asleep. George and Gloria had watched her sleep peacefully for two hours before someone told them that they could go home and that when she wakened in the morning, we would be called.

Do you want to know what kind of berry it was? A pokeberry, which is indeed poisonous. The important point is that even though we survived this incident without any permanent damage or expense, it made us realize the need to have emergency numbers close at hand. Ever since, when we take a reservation, we ask the guest for the number of a person to call in case of emergency. It also emphasized the need to have adequate insurance coverage.

LIABILITY INSURANCE

Most people who own homes have homeowner's insurance. These policies are difficult for most people to read and should be gone over carefully with the insurance agent. In some cases, homeowner's insurance will cover up to two paying guests; in others, it will not. If you are planning to open only one room for guests or rent your apartment unhosted, check to see if your current insurance is sufficient. If not, you should either change carriers or consider additional liability insurance. Liability insurance covers any losses to a guest that occur from injury because of your negligence. For instance, a guest might suffer an adverse reaction to something you serve for breakfast that had gone bad, trip on a loose scatter rug, or slip on some ice that you forgot to salt. If the guest sues and wins, your homeowner's insurance may not cover this. Settlements in liability cases have gotten out of hand; and in many cases, claimants have won even without proving fault.

For a number of years, reservation services were able to provide very low-cost liability riders to their host homes. In the three years that we participated in such a plan, we knew of only one paid claim: to two women who tripped on a patch of ice on someone's doorstep in Alaska. But the insurance company stopped offering the policy. Currently, if your B&B meets your state's requirements for noncommercial accommodations, you can qualify for liability coverage through any reservation service that is a member in good standing of Bed & Breakfast Reservation Services Worldwide. As of fall 1986, the cost to each host home for coverage of three rooms was $150 annually for $1 million per insured location per incident. If more than three rooms are to be covered, there is a $50 charge for each additional room. Elevators and chair lifts are not covered, and there is a $500 deductible. Each participant in this group coverage receives a certificate of insurance. The main copy of the policy is at the reservation service. Buying comparable insurance independently, if you can get it, will cost over $1,000.

The deductible is a way that the insurance company says, "We're in this together. Please keep your house safe." By taking all necessary precautions for the safety, security, and comfort of your guests, you will greatly reduce your chances of becoming involved in a claims action. Your reservation service, during its home inspection, will also alert you to potential problems. If there are any, make sure to remedy them before you accept your first guest.

Inform Your Agent

It is important that your homeowner's insurance agent know that you are opening your home as a B&B and that you have or don't have additional coverage. Make sure that additional insurance does not jeopardize your current coverage. Many policies have a fine-print clause that says something like "If you increase your hazards without notifying this insurance company, your policy is null and void." For example, if you store dynamite in your garage without telling your agent and the garage blows up, and with it your house, your homeowner's insurance probably won't pay for it even if you have been paying for fire insurance for twenty years.

Trying to anticipate any wrinkle of being involved in B&B, we asked an agent if this might be considered increasing our hazards. His response was that it would be a good idea to get approval beforehand. We did this and found that as long as we were up front and could show our liability certificate, our insurance company was willing to continue our homeowner's policy without any stipulations or increase in price. The same thing may or may not happen to you; some insurance carriers are very conservative. If your carrier drops you, don't worry. There are many fine companies with good reputations willing to write your policy.

SETTING HOUSE RULES

A guest contract stating house rules as well as host responsibilities should be part of your normal procedure. Each guest should be given this upon arrival and asked to sign it. Without

Bed & Breakfast U.S.A., Ltd.

GUEST CONTRACT

Name of Guest _____

Work Address _____ Home Address _____

Home Telephone _____ Work Telephone _____

Does anyone in your party smoke? _____

Mind children? _____ Mind pets? _____

Have allergies? _____ To what? _____

On a special diet? _____ Foods prohibited _____

Name & phone of someone to call in emergency _____

PLEASE READ THE FOLLOWING RULES. YOUR SIGNATURE INDI-
CATES THAT YOU AND MEMBERS OF YOUR PARTY ACCEPT AND
WILL ABIDE BY THEM DURING YOUR STAY IN THE HOST'S HOME.

1. It is the guests' responsibility to provide their own transportation.
2. The guests shall pay any balance of payment due in cash or traveler's checks to the host upon arrival (including all applicable taxes).
3. The host family agrees to the guests' use of the room subject to
   payment of all charges. Included in the charge for the room are daily
   breakfasts which may include: cereal, eggs, coffee, tea, toast, rolls,
   juice, milk, and/or specialties of the house mutually agreed on by the
   guest and host. Breakfast hours will be set by the host. Breakfast is
   provided at no charge and if breakfast is not taken, there will be no
   reduction in charges for the room.
4. The use of the room and right of access to the host family's home are
   solely for the guest and others in the guest's party included in the
   advance reservation. No one else is permitted to have access to the
   host family's home or the room.
5. If the host family supplies the guest with a key, the guest shall return
   the key on or before the last day of the guest's stay with the host
   family. The guest shall not duplicate the key or permit it to be in the
   possession of another person not in the guest's party. If the key is
   lost or stolen, the guest shall promptly notify the host family and pay
   the expense of replacing the locks and keys should the host family
   deem replacement necessary.
6. Telephone use by a guest shall be limited to incoming calls, an
   occasional local call, and credit card calls or calls charged to their
   home telephones.

7. The guest assures the host family and Bed & Breakfast U.S.A., Ltd. that information supplied by the guest is accurate, true, and correct. The guest agrees that the host family's responsibility to supply a room, breakfast, and other services shall end if the guest:

   a. fails to make payment for the room;
   b. becomes intoxicated, unduly boisterous, or makes excessively loud noises after 11:00 P.M.;
   c. brings illegal drugs on to the premises of the host;
   d. engages in any illegal actions or otherwise violates the laws of the United States or the State of New York.

   The host family's sole responsibility upon the occurrence of any of these terminating events is to direct the guest to alternative lodgings. The host family shall retain the money paid by the guest for all charges anticipated for the original reservation. The expense of alternative lodgings will be the responsibility of the guest alone.

8. Cancellation made less than seven days before commencement of a reservation shall entitle the host to keep one night's stay. The host will return any additional deposit to the reservation service for refund to the guest. Should a guest choose to leave before the prearranged departure date, he is responsible for one more night's lodging cost than the number of nights stayed. Additional days must be arranged with the host's permission and Bed & Breakfast U.S.A., Ltd. must be notified. Future visits must be booked through Bed & Breakfast U.S.A.

9. The guest acknowledges that the sole function of Bed & Breakfast U.S.A., Ltd. is to introduce the host and guest to each other. The host family is solely responsible for the room and services.

Guest Signature _____ *Date* _____

- -

GUEST RECEIPT

_____ has accepted accommodations in my B&B, subject to the terms of the guest contract provided and paid total charges including all deposits, fees, and taxes of $ _____ (U.S.)

_____ Arrival Date_____ (Host)

_____ Departure _____ (Address)

_____ Date Today _____

one, you run the risk of being not only misunderstood but sometimes taken advantage of by guests who think they are renting your personal services as well as your room. Dissatisfaction on the part of both guest and host most commonly arises when the type of accommodation is not clearly spelled out, when there is failure to state mutually accepted house limits, or when guests confuse a B&B with a hotel or motel. Your reservation service may provide this contract for you. On pages 98–99 you will find a sample guest contract used by Bed & Breakfast U.S.A. hosts. You can write yours to your particular circumstances.

SECURITY

If you feel uncomfortable about giving out the only key to your home, there are two simple solutions: (1) Add additional locks for use when you have no guests. When you have guests, use only the lock to which you have given guests the key. (2) Install a combination lock that can be reprogrammed. Give guests the current combination, and show them how to operate it. When these guests leave, enter a new combination.

In addition to door locks, you will want to advise your guests of any other security measures you normally employ, such as a burglar alarm system, direct-dial arrangements to local police departments with or without an audible signal from an alarm, and window locks (especially important for fire safety). If you do not wish to provide details of your home security system to guests, you may choose to stay up and admit guests personally. Be aware, however, that this works only for overnight guests. One of my hosts had two women stay for a week. One was attending an art workshop; the other had come just for vacation and to keep her friend company. By the second day, the vacationer called to see if there were other accommodations available because she felt that the host was shooing her out in the morning and waiting up for them at night, all because he didn't feel that they could understand the alarm system. By no means should guests be made to feel that they must be out of the house all day or plan their schedule according to that of the host. Arrival times must always be mutually decided on, but after that, guests should be able to come and go at will.

Here are other steps hosts may take to ensure security:

- Refrain from placing promotional brochures or business cards in public locations unless you put only your reservation service's phone number and no street address on this literature so that guests will be screened.

- Record the license plate number and make and model description of cars driven by guests. (This may be entered in a register separate from your guest book.)

- Telephone your reservation service at once if you notice anything out of line about the guests.

- Report any unacceptable behavior of a guest to the reservation service to prevent this guest from being referred to you or any other hosts in the network again.

- Discuss guest policies with all family members, including children, so that everyone knows what the guest is welcome to do in your home and which areas are the family's private domain.

To date, the screening policies of professional reservation services have resulted in six years of B&B hosting in the U.S. with no known incidents involving jeopardy to anyone's personal security. Breakage or damage to a host's home or other property has been less than that one anticipates from family members. Thefts are virtually unheard of. (More frequently, a guest leaves something behind.) These facts translate into a very low cost of insurance for hosts.

There is one consequence of operating a B&B that may strike you as negative. Once neighbors have been informed that you are opening your home to paying guests, there may be a drop in their ordinary protectiveness toward your home. They may become nonchalant about reporting strangers seen about your premises, for instance, because they presume that any such visitors are anticipated and welcome. This may be less of a problem if you host infrequently and can let your neighbors know when you have plans to do it.

If a neighbor complains, keep in mind that hosting results in fewer visitors overall and fewer cars competing for parking than most other customary home occupations. Because visitors have been screened for compatibility with you and your family, they are probably just the type of people that your neighborhood wants to welcome.

❖❖❖❖❖❖❖

Question: Though I enjoy entertaining at home and have done a good deal of it, I'd like some tips on handling the first few minutes after a guest arrives, particularly for the first time in my home. Should any business be transacted then, or should it wait until the guest is ready to depart?

Answer: Bed & Breakfast U.S.A. recommends that all business be transacted within the first twenty minutes of a guest's arrival. Some people feel awkward about money matters after they have spent some time with guests and gotten to like them. The reservation service will have briefed the guest to expect to pay upon arrival, so it won't come as a surprise.

A reprint compiled for hosts with the help of Kate Peterson of B&B Rocky Mountains points up what experienced hosts may do to make the arriving guest feel at home and welcome.

THE GIFT OF HOSPITALITY

1. Show room and house and give guests an opportunity to unload their belongings.
2. Offer a drink/beverage and ask if anything else is needed.
3. Take care of business (collecting money, signing guest contract and guest register, giving receipt) within twenty minutes of guest's arrival.
4. Answer questions and mention local attractions.
5. Supply an information sheet containing questions and answers about the area.
6. Collect brochures about area attractions and have them available.
7. Offer breakfast in bed, if desired (some B&B's charge extra for this).
8. Collect menus from a variety of popular area restaurants and clippings of restaurant reviews from local newspapers. Place in a folder available to guests.
9. Show guests where books, magazines, and newspapers are kept for their use.
10. Have good maps available: your region, your city, and your neighborhood (the latter with your house circled or highlighted for the guest's convenience in finding the way back at the end of the day).
11. Copy your local map with restaurants, movies, and attractions circled. Make enough copies so each guest can take one to keep. A simple promotional touch: use your business stationery to have your B&B address, telephone, and illustration/logo at the top.
12. Put umbrellas you are willing to lend in a stand near the front door and tell guests about it.
13. Collect articles from newspaper tourism and events sections. Copy them and keep in folder easily available for guests. Copies hold up better than newsprint originals.
14. Collect discount and promotional coupons from nearby attractions and restaurants (evenings when there are specials on the menu, etc.) and leave them out for guests to use.
15. If it's all right with you for guests to use your deck or patio for eating, leave a list of places where take-out food is available in town or those that deliver to the home. Remind guests that payment in cash is always necessary for food delivered to them.
16. Make copies of your breakfast specialty recipes in case guests would like to try them again when they arrive home. Again, using your business stationery will remind them of their visit whenever the recipe is used.
17. Set up a game corner or game shelf (garage sales can be treasure troves for these).

18. Tell your guests where they can find extra towels, more pillows or blankets, and the like. Let them know they should ask if they can't find something they need.

19. Invite guests to use the kitchen to boil hot water for tea or coffee or to place foods needing refrigeration or freezing away. Kitchen privileges for meal preparation are not part of your B&B responsibility to your guests; but if someone is staying more than a few days, you may opt to permit the use of your appliances and kitchenware as you see fit.

20. Place a welcoming tray in the guest room: fruit bowl, iced water or tea, drinking glass, mints, liqueur for after dinner relaxation, a pretty napkin, one or two cut flowers from your garden, a deck of cards.

21. When guests arrive, find out what they like to drink in the morning and make coffee or tea early for those who drink it. A thermos outside the door so the first cup of the day can be drunk in bed is a real treat for those who enjoy it..

22. Place sample sizes of toilet articles in drawers of guest room.

23. If you have a historic home, guests may like to learn about it. You may want to take a course about tracing its history and keep the results of your work available for guests to read if interested.

24. Check with your library, historical society, or neighborhood association about the availability of walking tours, published so people can take them on their own.

25. If your setting is conducive to romance, offer your guests some private time in front of the fireplace with a complimentary decanter of cognac or wine and the use of your music system.

26. In cold climates, flannel sheets are a nice winter's touch.

27. If you have a special interest or hobby which others might enjoy sharing as participants or observers, invite them to join you. Let guests know you as an individual, your way of life, your part of the country, but don't convey the impression that the guest is there to amuse you. Be available at breakfast or in the early evening for those who want to talk, but recognize when a guest wants privacy.

28. Keep an up-to-date list of service people in town (for example, in the event of broken eyeglasses, lost keys, spills on evening clothes, late night pharmacy needs, copying of a business report, typing services, babysitters, pet services).

29. Take out a membership in the local video rental shop if you allow guests to use your VCR equipment, or if you occasionally invite guests to join your family for a movie at home.

30. Provide a bedtime snack: cookies and milk, biscuits and hot chocolate, fortune cookies and wine, herb tea and scones, etc. This is particulary thoughtful for people who have had very late days at a hospital, nursing home, or funeral home and may have missed meals along the way.

❖❖❖❖❖❖

Question: Will I need to be able to accept credit cards from my guests?

Answer: *After being in business close to a year, I lost a large booking because the guest wanted to pay by credit card and we couldn't accept it. Since plastic of any type has always been repugnant to me and certainly one of the reasons B&B was so attractive was the lack of plastic associated with it, I had never tried to become a credit card merchant. But once this $1,000 booking slipped away, I knew the day had come to concede and apply for this privilege. I say "privilege" because that is the bank's attitude toward allowing you to help them make money. I naturally called my own bank first and was po-litely told by the manager that the bank had a policy that home-based businesses could not qualify to be credit card merchants. I then called every bank in Westchester County and New York City, only to be told the same thing. Having wasted close to a full day on this fool's errand, I became de-pressed and gave up temporarily.*

Shortly afterward I saw a story on a cable TV show about a business that allowed people to use their credit cards to pay for over-the-phone sexually explicit talk. I was outraged that this business was qualified to be a credit card merchant but my reservation service was not. I called the local chapter of the Association for Homebased Businessses and was told by the chapter president that she is a credit card merchant because an exception was made by her bank after her husband threat-ened to move his million-dollar account to another bank if his wife's company was not made eligible to accept credit cards. Well, even if my husband had had a million-dollar account at a bank, I didn't think that this type of blackmail should be necessary. My rage mounted, and I started calling state legis-lators and the small-business administration. I threatened that if someone didn't take action, I would take my story to television. *Within the week, the Union National Bank in Albany agreed to take my company on as a credit card merchant. They came to Croton and installed our credit card acceptance device in the reservation service office.*

When people call the reservation service less than a week before their stay, we arrange for them to pay by credit card. This helps to ensure that they are serious about using their reservations. After many years of experience, we have found that no matter how nice someone sounds over the telephone, if they don't pay in advance, they are likely not to show up. Big hotels overbook because they know exactly what percentage will be no-shows. But a host with one to four guest rooms can't afford one no-show and can't overbook under any circumstance.

It is not likely that a small B&B will be granted the ability to take credit cards, but your reservation service definitely should.

❖❖❖❖❖❖❖

Question: I have chosen a wonderful, very large house in a community that seems very receptive to my opening it to guests. I am terrified about decorating it. Can you give me any tips?

Answer: *For those who have lived in a home for a long time, raised a family there, and now plan to start a B&B, there may be little more to do than touching up the paint, buying some new sheets, and selecting a few plants. With a new home (even if its an older building), you will have to evaluate its needs, assess your budget, and proceed from there.*

My own story should provide a helpful example. We weren't in the million-dollar house market, and decorating the house on a limited budget was a challenge to be tackled without decorator assistance. My decorating talents were a good eye for color and texture and knowledge gleaned from many magazine articles about how to make a small room appear larger. Moving into a house with high ceilings and rooms twenty-seven to thirty-five feet long forced some new insights on us. I owe one of the best to my Aunt Francine, who was one of the people who looked at the house when we first bought it and saw, as we did, how wonderful it would look when we finally finished decorating. She immediately offered me her dining room table and chairs, which had been in storage for seventeen years. I asked her how she could justify paying to store something for so long. She said, "My dear, husbands come and go, but furniture is forever!" She should know, she's had three.

I traveled down to southern Jersey, where the storage company loaded the table and chairs on the truck, and happily rode back with my new treasures. When my husband arrived home from work that evening, we carried them in, only to find that a fifty-four-inch-long oval cherry table looked ridiculously small in the middle of a twenty-seven-foot-long dining room. This table now sits in the bay window, where I use it as a dessert buffet. So, decorating lesson 1: Large houses dwarf furniture. Although you now need to buy large pieces, this is not necessarily bad news. Very few homes can accommodate pieces of the size you need, so they are often available at garage and estate sales or auctions for a reasonable price.

I found that my home has rooms that look into each other through many open doorways. Therefore, my choice of colors had to be fairly similar so they wouldn't clash. Wallpaper is a fast way to achieve spectacular looks yet provide continuity. I selected three different patterns (one for each room) from the same color family. Originally, my front hall had white and gold flocking and was quite reminiscent of a Victorian brothel. The living room and dining room were in the same drab gray textured paper, which added to the look of being a large empty barn. Victorian houses have carved woodwork, leaded windows, turrets, and other features that require some formality in the main rooms. Country Americana looked out of place except perhaps on our sun porch. To fit in with the formality, I used vinyl moiré wallpapers in the living and dining rooms and a floral print in the front entry hall.

To make these large rooms look cozy, it was necessary to group the furniture into smaller subgroups. I removed the wall-to-wall carpeting, had the hardwood floors sanded and sealed, and bought oriental area rugs that helped define the smaller areas. A decorator told me that this technique is now referred to as "having a series of episodes."

We did the upstairs guest rooms one at a time. The largest we furnished with large Victorian pieces, with marble-topped dressers and a settee. The other B&B rooms developed over time as demand for them grew. Having four rooms, we put twin beds in one. (Twin beds are in less demand generally; but when clients need them, doubled bedded rooms just won't do.) To accommodate the beds, it was necessary to wall over one of the closets. When we grew from two to four rooms, we flew up to Maine, rented a truck, antiqued our way through country lanes, and came home with two rooms of country furniture at quite reasonable prices.

If you buy antique beds, they are almost always too short. Get a carpenter or handyman to extend the side boards six inches so you can accommodate a normal mattress and box spring. Always purchase new, firm mattresses. Very few people like soft ones, and most bed complaints are because a bed isn't firm enough. Remember to ask people if they are over six feet tall; most old beds have footboards that make for much discomfort if a person has no room to stretch out.

We have done each bedroom in a different color, varying the style to suit the size of the room. Your decor is a reflection of your unique personality and should remain so. One hostess I visited recently had bookshelves in each room. One room contained only mysteries, another romances, another classics, and so on. My rooms reflect Victorian romance, with candles, old-fashioned candies, and a decanter with brandy for each guest on their first night with us. Literature about the area and a train schedule in case they wish to visit New York City are also in each room.

Little extras are very memorable. Displayed collections are often focal points in a decorating scheme. Many hosts favor holiday and seasonal variations. Some hosts use fresh flowers or plants. At Christmastime, I decorate each room for the holidays, as well as the staircase and each of the tables downstairs. At breakfast, I try to feature seasonal foods, and I use butter molds to shape my butter pats into hearts, flowers, pumpkins, turkeys, and so on. It always surprises me that people rarely say anything about the Victorian antiques (I guess they expect them in a house like ours) but never fail to remark about the butters. Cloth napkins are also a nice touch. For guests who stay more than one night, I offer a choice of napkin rings shaped like little animals so that they will rec-ognize their napkins the next day. This also saves on laundry, since most napkins will stay fresh for a number of days. The guests also get a kick out of choosing their rings. My little pig is the favorite; someone at the table always knows who is sup-posed to have him.

Decorating your B&B should be fun both for you to do and for your guests to enjoy. If you feel decorating is not one of your strong points, you might want to call in a friend whose deco-rating appeals to you. Remember, this is your home first and therefore should be a place where you feel comfortable. If your taste is contemporary, don't feel that you have to change your house into country Americana for guests. As long as you do it with love and describe it accurately to prospective guests, those who come will not be disappointed.

6

**Public Relations
and Advertising**

Any business requires a combination of public relations (PR) and advertising to get it off the ground, and both are necessary to keep an established business before the public eye and perpetuate demand for it.

PUBLIC RELATIONS

An article on Bed and Breakfast in a major magazine is often the result of PR efforts by a reservation service or a collective effort of a number of them. In each article, certain B&B's will be featured, usually ones appropriate to the readership of that particular magazine. No one can pay to be included in the story. What goes into the story is an editorial decision made by the magazine. How, then, can a service's PR be responsible? The service may have sent in the story outline with pictures of sample B&B's for an editor to look at or invited the editor to lunch or a hosted get-together and suggested the article. They may have made a speech or given a radio interview that caught an editor's ear and then provided information when that editor inquired about B&B. The service may send press releases about an interesting event such as a gourmet or mystery weekend.

The Seed-Planting Approach

I personally follow the *seed-planting approach* to public relations. This involves doing something every day that may result in letting the public know about my agency or the joys of Bed and Breakfast. It is called *seed planting* because as in gardening, some of the effort pays off this season, some in the future, and some not at all. Attending a chamber of commerce meeting to hand out business cards and brochures, speaking to a fraternal organization or a business group, or calling a corporation to set up an appointment with its travel or personnel department might be my PR activity for the day. Sending Christmas cards to my guests with short personal notes is also PR because the cards will remind them of an enjoyable stay and perhaps encourage them to visit my B&B again or recommend it to a friend headed this way.

Professional Firms

There are companies that specialize in getting information about your business into the papers and magazines and onto TV and radio talk shows. They write your press releases, coach you for interviews, and so on. They are professionals who expect to be well paid for their efforts. Some contracts pay according to how often you are mentioned. This may or may not relate to how much business you do as a consequence.

Many PR professionals believe that it takes at least seven exposures for the average listener to understand a new concept. So public relations is not a one-shot deal. Rather, it is a continual effort to expose new clients to your product, create a demand for it, and make sure they come to you to buy it. If the publicity is positive, it may help you achieve all three. There are no guarantees, however. You may invite a travel writer to spend a night at your B&B gratis and then wait months to see the story. Perhaps the article will not even mention your B&B or have something negative to say about your decor, your breakfast, or something else. Or the writer's editor may need space for a paid ad and cut the paragraph about your home. Should this risk discourage your efforts? No.

Doing It Yourself

If you do not use a PR firm, you will have to act as your own publicist. The true cost of public relations efforts both in money and in personal time expended varies greatly. Some costs are direct, such as membership dues for a trade group, a reservation service, or a chamber of commerce. In these cases, you know what the cost is, but there may be a tremendous variation in what each group does for your business. Sometimes the results vary from year to year or season to season. Moreover, it may depend on whether you merely pay dues or also participate by attending meetings, volunteering for committees, and so on.

Many of your efforts may not produce direct business immediately, and it can be difficult to keep up your efforts in the absence of direct results. I have done many TV shows. My preparation for taping can take days, and the taping itself takes hours. But the final edited feature may be aired for less than five minutes. Although thousands of people may see the show, only two or three may follow through by calling to make a reservation. I justify the energy expended by assuring myself that such appearances are one of the seven exposures and that by promoting B&B in general, I am helping to build the demand for everyone in the industry. Successful entrepreneurs learn this early. The consistent and repeated mentions of Bed & Breakfast U.S.A. in stories about B&B are part of what has built our good reputation and why newcomers to this type of travel call us when they decide to make reservations.

ADVERTISING

Advertising is the buying of space in print media or air time on TV or radio to promote your name and product. Because you are the purchaser, you decide exactly what will be said about you. You pay for your own artwork and have final say about copy. Depending on how much you pay, you can decide whether your message will be on a particular page or time slot. You also know precisely when and for how long your ad will run. But the public also knows that you have paid for this message and, therefore, may take what you have to say about yourself with a grain of salt.

Advertising agencies have graphic artists, layout people, copywriters and editors, and years of experience in knowing which vehicles have produced the best results. They are the professionals in this field, and they expect to be paid professional fees for services rendered. The price of advertising is often related to how many people can be expected to read or hear it. What may seem an outrageous cost for placing an ad in a magazine or newspaper with a large circulation can be justified by the very low per capita expenditure that exposure in such a publication guarantees.

The cost of an ad varies according to the circulation of the vehicle, the size of the ad, how many insertions you commit yourself to in advance, whether or not you supply camera-ready copy, and other factors. You will generally pay more to place your ad in a paper or magazine with a large circulation or exclusive clientele. The larger your ad, the more it will cost, but you will usually pay less per square inch. If you decide on a series of ads placed each week, month, or issue, your cost per ad will usually be less. Camera-ready copy is copy that can be run exactly as submitted, for which you have already silk-screened the photos, typeset the copy, and had your graphic artist do the sketch, layout, and border. If you are buying a two-by-three-inch space, your ad is submitted in that size. The term is usually applied only to *display ads*, that is, ads that are placed throughout a publication, usually interspersed with articles. *Classified ads* are found grouped together in a special section and are considerably less expensive. Like public relations, advertising is something you do, not once, but repeatedly so that your clients will be able to locate you when they need to.

PUBLICITY AND ADVERTISING FOR A BED AND BREAKFAST

Are you saying to yourself, "This sounds like a lot of money and a full-time job"? You're right. Hotels have people on staff whose total job is to plan and execute these tasks. A small B&B with fewer than six rooms would very seldom bring in enough money to justify such expenses. Still, without publicity and advertising, no one will come to your B&B. In many cases, this is where your reservation service really earns its commissions. Many big businesses spend up to 40 percent of gross sales on sales and promotion, and a business trying to increase sales will spend more than a business trying to maintain sales. A new business needs all the help it can get.

Helping Your Reservation Service to Promote You

When selecting a reservation service to represent you, one of the many things you will want to know about is what kind of advertising and promotion it has done in the past and plans to do in the future. (Before choosing a reservation service, please read Chapter 7, "Working with a Reservation Service," carefully.) If a reservation service is new, you may help it to plan its strategies in this area. By volunteering to attend meetings, give speeches, or allow your home to be featured in an article, you can increase the demand for your B&B. Many reservation services ask their hosts for one free night if a travel writer wants to sample their B&B's. If you are asked, accept and do your best to see that they get a good impression, but don't try to overwhelm. Travel writers are nobody's fools and will usually be quite able to see the advantages of a B&B by themselves.

Become a local representative for your service. Distribute brochures to restaurants, friends, professional associates, local real estate salespeople, local corporations, women's centers, schools, catering services (who may refer guests to you when catering large events such as weddings with many out of town guests), funeral directors, maternity shops, nursery schools, senior citizen's centers, hospital auxiliaries, and so on.

Let your reservation service know about events that will take place in your area as far in advance as possible. It sometimes takes three to six months to properly promote travel for an upcoming event. And be sure to keep your service informed about any changes in your household or B&B accommodations. If you get a cat, don't forget to share this news. An allergic guest sent to you based on an earlier report of having no pets will cause problems for the guest, may cause you to have to refund the money for the stay, and puts your service in the position of having misrepresented you to guests. If you get a canopy bed or antique bed linens, let your service know so that it can use these special features to entice couples looking for a romantic getaway.

The Guidebooks

There are at least two dozen B&B guides currently available to the traveling public. Most list homes that the authors have never seen or inspected. The hosts have filled out a form, and most have paid a fee to be listed. A safe way to increase your exposure to travelers while protecting your privacy and continuing to avail yourself of your reservation service's screening is to list your B&B in a few of the better guidebooks, leaving out your street address and giving your reservation service's phone number.

For those of you who belong to one of these reservation services (See the appendix of Worldwide members for a list of reservation services), you may also have the opportunity to go on the Delta Airlines Computer System. This system is accessed by 3,000 travel agencies across the U.S. and in 9 countries abroad. There are some nominal costs to hooking up with this system and a very low service charge from Delta for each reservation booked.

Setting Up Your Press Kit

Be careful when putting together any material, be it a business card, a brochure, or letterhead stationery. Think about who will receive it and whether you want to have your address available to unscreened travelers. Cautious hosts often include only a reservation service phone number on business cards and brochures. The reason the security record of reservation services has been so good is that they send hosts screened guests who have made and paid for reservations in advance. These are not the average hotel or motel guests who pull off the road when tired.

When guests call a reservation service to ask for a booking at a specific B&B, that is precisely where the service will try to book them. Your service may have affiliate's cards for your use, or you may have a designer do a drawing of your B&B for personalized cards. Logos are also a popular attention-getting device. Try to get some reliable advice about what looks good. Pen-and-ink sketches of your home usually reproduce well and are very effective eye-catchers. Printing can be quite an investment, so you don't want to have to reprint too often.

116

Here is a sample business card.

```
┌─────────────────────────────────────────────┐
│                                               │
│             Barbara's B&B                     │
│                                               │
│      Victorian elegance in the village of     │
│              Croton-on-Hudson.                 │
│                                               │
│      Please call Monday through Friday         │
│            10:00 A.M. to 4:00 P.M.             │
│              (914) 271-6228.                   │
│                                               │
│      A member of Bed & Breakfast U.S.A., Ltd.  │
│                                               │
└─────────────────────────────────────────────┘
```

Your cards, however, are only one piece of a press kit. A press kit also contains:

- A one-page summary of what B&B is and the specifics of yours.

- Photographs of the exterior of your house and at least one guest room. Black and white photos are preferable to color in case someone wants to reproduce them in a newspaper or magazine article. (As you can afford it, you will want to build a file of professional photos of your B&B.)

- A short (one-page) interview explaining your interests, what has attracted you to B&B, your community involvements, and the like.

- An information sheet on your reservation service explaining how to make a reservation.

- A copy of one article about B&B nationally.

- A folder to hold these inserts. Your business card should be attached to the front of the folder.

The press kit is what you give to business people who ask for information or to members of the press before they come to interview you or before you appear as an invited expert on B&B. Bed and Breakfast is still a novelty in much of the country, so being a well-prepared spokesperson is a good reflection on the industry.

Your Brochure

You may not feel that it is necessary to have a brochure describing your B&B. If you accept guests only through your reservation service, it will usually describe your offering in its catalog. But if you decide to create a brochure, include the specialties you offer. For example, this is the place to let guests know that trout fishing instruction is available by arrangement. Include your breakfast hours and whether you offer a full or continental breakfast. If there are house rules or restrictions, they belong here, too. Your brochure should be a reflection of your style and consistent with the atmosphere of your B&B. Indicate that you are a member of a reservation service, and if your service is part of Bed & Breakfast Services Worldwide, use Worldwide's logo somewhere on your brochure, since the logo is used in public service pieces about high-quality B&B and you will want to associate yourself with this group.

❖❖❖❖❖❖❖

Question: There are many off-season periods when very few guests want to come to my area. I am intrigued by the idea of planning special events in association with other B&B's. What should I expect to do with my reservation service to get this started?

Answer: Talk with your service, travel and tourism bureau, community affairs department of a local college, sports and hobby interests. Most reservation services need a minimum of three to six months lead time to properly promote an event in directories or newsletters sent to guest members. Planning such events for your area's slowest season helps even out B&B business for hosts. Successful promotions B&B's have organized have included bicycle tours on weekdays, with guests biking between participating B&B's to see fall foliage; a gourmet weekend, with each participating B&B responsible for preparing and serving a different meal or party; bridge blitzes scheduled for long February weekends (an interesting option for nonskiers bound for ski areas as companions to people who can't be kept off the slopes or for areas where there is no skiing); singles holiday celebrations; tennis tournaments; investors' seminars; and astrology sessions. One hostess I represent offers candlelight dinners for two in her guest rooms during January and February. The only limitations here are your imagination and energy. Reservation services are becoming increasingly skilled at aiding organizers in coordinating complex reservations involving several B&B's and several events. As Reservation Services become more and more visible throughout the travel industry via computer linkages with travel agents, special events planning is likely to become more significant in increasing B&B business.

7

❖❖❖❖❖❖❖❖❖❖❖❖❖❖❖❖❖❖❖ 7 ❖❖❖❖❖❖❖❖❖❖❖❖❖❖❖❖❖❖❖

Working with a Reservation Service

The leaps-and-bounds growth of private-home Bed and Breakfast across North America is largely attributable to one unique aspect: the professional reservation services. Although it is possible to operate a B&B as an independent host, it is hard to come up with a reason why anyone would choose not to work with a quality reservation service.

RECOGNIZING A NEED

The industry's pioneers saw the need for private-home B&B's in America. They founded reservation services to encourage people to open their homes. Each service is an independent business, not a franchise. The founders come from diverse backgrounds. Most are well educated, have worked in service industries in the past, or been educators.

The grass-roots B&B movement encouraged progress at different speeds in different parts of the country. For the most part, reservation services developed regionally, too. Being close to the homes they represented made it possible for the services to inspect each home and investigate any complaint. Thus, a service could represent high standards and assure quality control. They knew the attractions of the area as well as the diverse accommodations nearby.

PRESERVING HOST-HOME INDIVIDUALITY

Reservation services also saw the importance of assuring high standards without interfering with how hosts managed their B&B's. The appeal of B&B is dependent on the individuality of each host home that results from diversity of personality, architecture, and decorating style. At the same time, homes could agree to provide clean, pleasant accommodations and a hearty American breakfast and to share their expertise about their region with guests. Reservation services thus came to stand for high quality while preserving the unique blends of style, personality and menu that make B&B's so attractive.

SPECIALIZATION VERSUS A BROADER APPROACH

I have been to many national meetings of reservation service leaders. The first one I attended was an American Bed & Breakfast Association Meeting of East Coast Reservation Services in Washington, D.C., early in 1983. Each of us talked about how to solve the same questions: How to screen travelers, develop host homes, and work with local and state governments to clarify rules and regulations that could affect the growth of this new industry.

As the meeting progressed, it became very clear to me that each reservation service had its own philosophy. One listed only historic homes. Another listed only homes that could accept guests who arrived by boat. Both were a far cry from my broader thinking that a B&B can be a simple room in a normal home convenient to something people want to attend. Others might want something unusual, historic, or deluxe, accommodations interesting in their own right. All, if clean, comfortable, and appropriately priced would attract their own segments of the traveling public. Although there are still agencies that focus on very specialized travelers (for example, a reservation service that plans canoe trips in conjunction with overnight stays at B&B's), most offer a wide variety of accommodations.

REGIONAL LIMITATIONS

Despite the positive aspects of regionally defined reservation services, problems soon developed. Making reservations was complicated. A traveler on an extended trip needed to call a number of services in order to pull the whole trip together. Travelers who read a complimentary article about their local reservation service would call and ask to make reservations at B&B's across the country. But because of the service's regional limitations, it was forced to refer these travelers to other services without knowing if the referral was acted on by the traveler. Statistics made it clear that most travelers who could not be helped by the reservation service they called did not call a second agency and went back to their traditional way of traveling.

RESERVATION SERVICES EXPAND THEIR SCOPE

To keep from losing both types of travelers, services expanded their scope from bookings within their own networks to homes listed with affiliate services. Bed & Breakfast Reservation Services Worldwide was organized in April of 1985 to set standards that services could agree on so that each could feel comfortable about relying on others to inspect and follow through on homes that they all would now be sending clients to. To offset the added cost of doing long-distance business, many services became membership organizations, charging a reservation fee or annual membership to guests.

MEMBERSHIP BENEFITS HOST AND GUEST

Such a membership works out well. Once guests have it, they are more likely to try Bed and Breakfast again rather than traditional accommodations. The more they use the membership, the better the value they receive. The more often guests use a service, the better it knows them and what pleases them, and this knowledge helps the service to provide better matches of hosts and guests. Networking among services also increases the exposure of each host home because services across the country know about them. The reservation fees or membership dues help to offset increased telephone costs, and the reservation services involved split the commission for each stay.

RESERVATION SERVICES BENEFIT HOST HOMES

Reservation services have become a recognizable force in the travel industry through the formation of Bed & Breakfast Services Worldwide and computer linkage with travel consultants. They enable more people to stay at B&B's and more hosts to do business. The services provide a myriad of benefits to their members, from being advocates of private-home B&B to legislatures, regulatory bodies, and the media to screening both hosts and guests and relieving hosts of much time-consuming work so that they are better able to enjoy having guests.

Advocacy

Your reservation service has probably been instrumental in clarifying state and local rules and regulations. Often, they have helped point out inconsistencies between government agencies or conflicting state and local rules. Bed & Breakfast U.S.A., Ltd., fought and won a zoning battle in Croton-on-Hudson that established a legal precedent in New York State for classifying B&B as a "customary home occupation" appropriate in residential neighborhoods. The findings of this trial have been shared with many other B&B hosts across the nation for use in similar zoning cases.

Education

Services educate hosts by running seminars and holding meetings to keep them up-to-date on issues relevant to the growth of the industry and their individual businesses. In addition, as part of their publicity efforts, reservation services have educated the American public about the joys of B&B. This has created the demand that is helping the industry grow rapidly.

Education also includes sending guests tips for being a good guest that stress the differences between a B&B and a hotel. Below is a sample of this type of educational piece.

Public service messages written by Bed & Breakfast Reservation Services Worldwide are educating travelers about staying at a B&B for the first time. Guests unfamiliar with the more

---

SAY YES TO BEING A GOOD GUEST

Book Early: You will have your choice of places to stay. Reservation services have business hours. Make sure you call during those times. Otherwise, you will probably have to call again or accept a collect call.

Call Ahead: Your host needs to know when to expect you. In private-home accommodations, hosts have many outside activities and no staff. It is very frustrating to have to stay at home all day waiting for a guest to arrive who hasn't had the courtesy to call ahead. Try to call at least forty-eight hours in advance. Your host will be ready to welcome you.

In Case of Delay: Call to let your host know your change in arrival time.

Find Out About Breakfast: Let your host know if you have any special requirements, food preferences, or allergies. Different hosts have different rules about breakfast hours. It is a good policy to check at arrival with your host to determine when breakfast is served.

Beds: Always indicate your prefrence about type of bed, and let your reservation service know if anyone is over six feet tall. Most antique beds have footboards that can cause considerable discomfort for tall sleepers.

Respect Other Guests: If you are sharing a bath, tidy up after yourself so the next guest finds the bathroom as clean as you did. Make sure to bring a robe, since even B&B's with private baths very seldom have access to the bath without leaving your room.

If you come in late, remember that others are already asleep, and keep your voices down.

Deposits: Deposits are always necessary to reserve a B&B. Hosts often have only a few rooms, and holding a room for someone is taken seriously. Your deposit shows that you are taking the reservation seriously, too.

Balance of Payment: Expect to pay any balance due plus applicable sales tax upon arrival in cash or traveler's checks.

Cancellations If circumstances force you to cancel a reservation, don't delay in informing your host and the reservation service. When booking, check to see how far in advance you can cancel without paying a penalty. Most places will charge at least a day's cost for cancellations made after designated dates. Certain places have no-refund policies at special times of the year.

Get to Know Your Hosts! They are an important reason you've chosen B&B travel. They know their locale well and are happy to share their expertise with you.

Send Back Your Evaluation Form: Reservation services use these for ongoing quality control and appreciate your reactions. By giving the service your feedback, you help it to serve you better.

In Return for Being a Good Guest: Your hosts will extend a warm welcome, personal attention, and gracious hospitality at reasonable rates and help to make your stay a memorable one and travel an enriching experience once again.

personal nature of B&B will understand and comply with respect and sensitivity toward hosts and fellow guests alike. This is very important as the industry's client base becomes broader.

Services also conduct regular seminars to encourage perspective hosts and to stimulate travelers to use B&B's. These seminars answer questions about start-up and management and keep hosts up-to-date on new regulations that may affect them. Slides and photographs of host homes are prominently featured at such meetings.

If you belong to a reservation service that belongs to the trade association, you will benefit from the power in numbers it represents. Whereas one person or family may have a difficult time getting the ear of someone in government, the media, or big business, a network that represents fifty, a hundred, or more citizens with similar interests can achieve its goals more easily. For example, by pooling our numbers nationally, member B&B's have access to low-cost liability insurance. Legislators see us as a voting bloc. Suppliers of linens and other goods see us as a purchasing bloc. It is important to be united and well organized in good times. That way, when there are difficulties for the industry, they can be faced together by a group already clear about its goals and usefulness to the public.

It is only by having strong organizations supporting and representing their interests that individual B&B's can have the power to fight other interests who seek to hamper their growth and success. For example, in 1986, the California Inn Association complained to the California Office of Tourism that private-home B&B's should not be represented in state tourism literature compiled by the California Lodging Association. On behalf of the Bed & Breakfast Reservation Services of California and their member hosts homes, Susan Morris, Executive Director of Bed & Breakfast Reservation Services Worldwide, wrote a letter to the California Office of Tourism explaining both what reservation services do for the traveler and how B&B's fill a need that brings more visitors and tourist dollars into the state. This is only the start of a unified drive to make the California Lodging Association understand that Bed and Breakfasts are part of the lodging industry, also.

Easier Access for Travel Professionals

In 1987, Bed & Breakfast Reservation Services Worldwide has made it possible for individual B&B's to be included on Delta Airlines' Delta Datas II Automated Reservation System. This provides travel agents in 3,000 offices across the United States and nine countries abroad with access to the B&B's represented by Worldwide's membership. The computerized system increases volume but directs reservation requests to your reservation service's computer and allows its staff to continue to match hosts and guests while protecting your privacy until the reservation is confirmed and deposits collected.

Promotion

As any reservation service will tell you, promotion never stops. Each year, services conduct local campaigns that are responsible for numerous features about Bed and Breakfast on radio, on television, in the newspapers, and in magazines. Often, this involves encouraging travel writers to use B&B's so that they, in turn, can introduce new audiences to the concept. Reservation service representatives may attend travel industry conferences and seminars for the same reason. Press releases are sent regularly to hundreds of newspapers, magazines, and radio stations. Most reservation service directors have also become extremely skilled at presenting the B&B story to business groups, civic associations and professional groups and at giving interviews and appearing on talk shows.

Bed & Breakfast U.S.A., Ltd. (just one reservation service, remember) spends over $1,000 annually on dues for membership in various chambers of commerce, convention and visitors' bureaus, B&B associations, business owner organizations, and other groups.

Cash outlays for direct advertising are also considerable. Each year, many thousands of dollars are spent to follow up articles written about B&B and make sure prospective guests know how to find us. This involves distributing brochures and directories in response to inquiries and maintaining an up-to-date mailing list of people interested in B&B. At Bed & Breakfast U.S.A., postage and printing alone (not to mention design, editorial, and layout) cost more than $10,000 a year. Other reservation services that diligently pursue this course incur similar expenses.

All this activity has put B&B in the public eye. Major stories have appeared in the following media (to name but a few):

- *The New York Times*
- *New York Daily News*
- *Chicago Tribune*
- *Women's Day* magazine
- *Ms.* magazine
- Gannett newspapers (*USA Today*)
- CBS TV
- NBC 6 and 11 O'Clock News in New York
- Cable News Network
- Independent News Network
- *Readers' Digest*
- WGY and WMCA radio
- The BBC

A COURTEOUS AND CONSCIENTIOUS OFFICE STAFF

Your reservation service provides a courteous and conscientious office staff to answer inquiries and match guests to host homes during regular business hours. A new service may start as a very small operation with part-time hours in the home of the director. As it grows, a staff is hired and adjusted to meet the seasonally fluctuating demand for accommodations. These are the people who take a lot of the clerical drudgery off your hands. They are there to answer calls so that you can lead a normal life and not worry about missing business.

You should have an answering machine so that the service can leave messages for you. You should answer these messages promptly because usually the service has only twenty-four hours to get back to a guest with a commitment about his or her reservation.

Correspondence

The service staff is also responsible for dealing with mail, processing deposits, and getting confirmation letters and fees out to you and your guests. When an effective promotional piece is published, hundreds of letters can pour into an office. Many just want general information about B&B, but all have to be answered. Any time you want to volunteer at your reservation service, your help will be gratefully accepted.

Credit Cards

It may be difficult, if not impossible, for a small private-home B&B to become a credit card merchant, but your reservation service can accept cards. This is important because when reservations are made at the last minute, the stay can be guaranteed by credit card payment, assuring that your room will be paid for and the cancellation policy enforced if the guest does not show up.

Screening

Reservation services take steps to assure that guests are reliable. The vast majority of B&B travelers are lovely people, but the screening process occasionally discloses unacceptable guests. For example, one caller gave Bed & Breakfast U.S.A. a prestigious Park Avenue address but admitted, when questioned further by the staff, that this was his mother's address. He gave his mother as a reference, so before arranging the booking for him, the service called her. She said we would have to take him at our own risk. Needless to say, we did not accept him.

Similarly, the reservation service is sensitive to hosts' attitudes. This is a major reason home visits are mandatory before a reservation service accepts a new B&B. This procedure is costly and time-consuming, but it is essential in assuring the public of the quality that services represent. Though it doesn't happen very often, there are some prospective hosts who are so insensitive to the needs of the guests that they do not belong in B&B. One prospective host asked me if it was really necessary to have anything to do with the guests. His house was beautiful, but his attitude was inconsistent with the B&B philosophy of gracious personal hospitality.

ONGOING QUALITY CONTROL

After a host is accepted by a reservation service, guests are sent rating sheets to be filled out and returned to the service at the conclusion of their stay. This provides constant follow-up. Hosts often learn how to improve their service, as a result of guests' comments. However, this information is not usually shared with hosts directly because most guests don't want to seem ungrateful. Also, this monitoring sometimes points out the need to make another home visit. If problems persist, a host is dropped.

Sample Rating Sheet
(Courtesy of B&B Rocky Mountains)

THANK YOU FOR STAYING WITH US! Your comments are valuable to us and help us to provide the type of Bed and Breakfast accommodations you want. We hope to see you again. Please do tell your friends about us. Please return this form to our office after your trip.

Your name _____ Host _____ Dates _____

Host Home (1 is poor; 10 is excellent; please circle one)

Cleanliness	1	2	3	4	5	6	7	8	9	10
Comfort	1	2	3	4	5	6	7	8	9	10
Cost	1	2	3	4	5	6	7	8	9	10
Convenience of location	1	2	3	4	5	6	7	8	9	10

Host

Courtesy	1	2	3	4	5	6	7	8	9	10
Friendliness	1	2	3	4	5	6	7	8	9	10
Helpfulness	1	2	3	4	5	6	7	8	9	10
Breakfast	1	2	3	4	5	6	7	8	9	10

Reservation Service

Courtesy	1	2	3	4	5	6	7	8	9	10
Promptness	1	2	3	4	5	6	7	8	9	10
Accurate Information	1	2	3	4	5	6	7	8	9	10

Would you stay with these hosts again?   Yes/No

Would you tell your friend's about us?   Yes/No

Additional Comments _____

_____

_____

_____ Please send information about gift certificates.

_____ Please send information to the travel planner at my business:

Name _____

Address _____

City/State/Zip _____

Telephone _____

Firm _____

I learned about staying B&B from a member host _____

_____ or another way (specify) _____

_____

COSTS OF REPRESENTATION

Belonging to a reservation service is not costly once you realize how much work is being done for you. For example, at Bed & Breakfast U.S.A., new hosts pay a $50 membership fee the first year and $25 in subsequent years. The additional $25 in the first year helps to offset some of the cost of making the home visit. A 20 percent commission is paid on each booking made through the service or resulting from its advertising or public relations efforts, including all returning guests and their referrals. If you elect to be on the Delta system, you will pay a one-time charge of $5 a room for our hookup charges plus a $15 annual fee to Delta and a $3-per-booking charge to Delta for reservations that come through its system. The reservation service pays a commission to the travel agent initiating the reservation through the Delta System.

Membership dues and the amount of the commission may vary slightly from service to service. Commissions usually range between 20 and 30 percent. The charge for $1 million of insurance is currently $150 for up to three rooms and $50 a room for more than three. This insurance has a $500 deductible and does not cover elevators or chair lifts. Liability insurance on an individual host home without this group policy could easily cost over $1,000.

SELECTING A RESERVATION SERVICE

There may be only one reservation service that covers your region or there may be many. You may not have to choose only one. Very few services are exclusive, and each understands that it may not be able to send you guests as often as you would like. All reservation services are not equal. To decide if a service can really help you function more efficiently and/or increase your business, ask some questions of the director before having a representative slate you for a home visit and interview. To help you do this, here is a questionnaire.

Reservation Service Questionnaire

	Yes	No
Does the service inspect all member homes?	____	____
Does the service promote each B&B?	____	____
Does it maintain a business office with regular hours for telephone service, and an answering machine?	____	____
Does the service help you determine the price to charge for your rooms?	____	____
Does it set and enforce a cancellation policy?	____	____
Is the reservation service quoted often about B&B in favorable press coverage?	____	____
Does it collect money (deposits) from guests?	____	____
Does the service share knowledge about pertinent B&B regulations in your state and area?	____	____
Does the service offer a group liability insurance policy for members to purchase?	____	____
Does it sponsor events for members to meet and to improve their hosting skills?	____	____
Does the service encourage networking by publishing newsletters or other communications?	____	____
Does the service belong to Bed & Breakfast Reservations Services Worldwide, the trade association that sets standards for the industry?	____	____
Does it have a computer hookup so that travel agents can gain access to all its listings, including your B&B?	____	____
Does the service have a reputation of consistent, courteous treatment of hosts and guests?	____	____
Will the service provide you with the names and telephone numbers of two or three current hosts as references?	____	____
Does the service revise its directory of host homes often enough to keep up-to-date with new listings and new developments at established homes?	____	____
Does the service check with the host before booking each guest?	____	____
Does the service offer special purchasing plans for linens and other items necessary for doing business?	____	____
Does the service offer member hosts a waiver of fees for booking reservations at other B&B's or similar courtesies?	____	____

If the answer to many of these questions is yes, you may be ready to apply for host status. Here is a sample host application. (It is the one used by Bed & Breakfast U.S.A., Ltd.)

Bed & Breakfast U.S.A., Ltd.

P.O. BOX 606 • CROTON-ON-HUDSON, NY 10520 • (914) 271-6228

NAME _____ PHONE (____) ____-_____

Street Address _____ City _____ State _____ Zip _____

Mailing Address (if different) _____

Members in household (if any children, include ages) _____

Will you accept children? Y N   Smokers? Y N   Do you or any member of your family smoke? Y N   Do you have pets? Y N   If yes, what kind? _____ How many? _____ How long have you lived in this home? _____ the area? _____ Where did you hear about B&B USA? _____

DESCRIPTION OF HOME: TYPE (e.g. Victorian, Colonial, etc.) _____

Year built _____ Describe (include unique features) _____

_____

_____ (Attach photos)

Circle extras in home (not guest rooms): PIANO, AC, TV, CABLE TV, VCR, POOL TABLE, POOL, JACUZZI, FIREPLACE, OTHER _____

LOCATION OF HOME BY CAR: Mins. to heart of nearest city? _____

What city? _____ Mins. to nearest restaurant? _____

How long to airport? _____ Train station? _____ Blocks to city bus? _____

Do guests need car? Y N

List attractions nearby with drivetime: _____

_____

HOST INFORMATION

Host Occupation _____ How long? _____

Company? _____ WK Phone _____

Spouse Occupation _____How long? _____

Company? _____ WK Phone _____

If retired, please give former occupation and write retired next to it.

What are your hobbies and interests? _____

_____

Have you travelled B&B?   Y   N   Where? _____ Breakfast you'll serve:

Full or Continental (circle one) Sample menu _____

USE THE FOLLOWING ABBREVIATIONS TO FILL IN THE CHART BELOW.
SIZE OF BED: K   (king),   Q   (queen),   TBD   (twin bedded double),
      S   (single bed).

TYPE OF BED: M/B   (mattress & boxspring),   Sofa   (sleeper couch),
      P   (platform bed),   WB   (waterbed),   C   (canopy),   4P   (four-
      poster),   B   (bunks),   T   (trundle),   H   (highriser).

BATHROOM: PA   (private attached),   P   (private access in hallway),
      Semi   (share with one other room),   SB   (share w/other guests),
      SF   (share w/family).

BATH: S   (shower),   T   (tub),   C   (combined shower and tub).

PLACEMENT OF ACCOMMODATION: 1   (lower level—stairs down),
      2   (first floor—no stairs),   3   (upstairs 1 flight),   4   (apart-
      ment building—indicate which floor and E if elevator building),
      also indicate DM if doorman building,   5   (3rd floor
      of private home).

AMENITIES: AC   (air conditioning),   TV   (black & white TV),   CTV
      (color TV),   K   (kitchenette),   suite   (includes sitting room),
      R   (rollaway), crib, (laundry facilities), canoe or boat,   HT   (hot
      tub),   S   (sauna),   D   (deck).   PE   (private entrance),   UnH
      (available unhosted),   FP   (fireplace in bedroom),   LK   (lock on
      bedroom door).

ROOM	SIZE BED	TYPE BED	BATHROOM	BATH	PLACEMENT	AMENITIES
A						
B						
C						

If you have more than three rooms, please indicate above information on a separate sheet.

ADDITIONAL THOUGHTS: Will you have complimentary beverages (coffee, tea, etc.) available for guests?   Y   N

Do you currently belong to any reservation service which sends paying B&B guests to you?   Y   N

If so which? _____ On a separate sheet of paper, please provide a detailed description of how to get to your home from the nearest highway or airport (if applicable). Locate your home on a map (hand drawn is OK or use a phone book map of the area). Be on time for interview (circle preference) Weekdays/Weekends   AM/PM

I understand that this application is only part of the information Bed & Breakfast USA, Ltd. requires to evaluate my request for host membership. A visit by a member of the staff will take place before an agreement is authorized. My $20.00 non-refundable interview/application fee is enclosed. This fee will be applied towards my first year's membership fee if accepted as a Bed & Breakfast USA, Ltd. host. The balance of my year's membership is due when the host contract is signed if accepted at the host visit. I understand that thereafter B&B USA will be entitled to a 20% commission on all guests sent through B&B USA, Ltd.

Signed _____ Date _____

THE HOME VISIT

To prepare for the home visit, the first thing you should do is relax. B&B hosting is a two-way street. Reservation services want good new hosts; they need the hosts' hospitality as much as the hosts need the services' marketing. The purpose of the home visit is for the reservation service to meet you and see what you've done with your home so that it can represent you accurately to prospective guests. You will be providing a very personal service, after all, as a joint venture with your reservation service. Both parties should feel comfortable with each other and be fully informed about what each will provide. Your house should be clean, pleasant, and ready to receive company. Set the table for breakfast for two, and make it attractive. Welcome the interviewer as you would a guest. The interview gives you a chance to ask questions and clarify day-to-day operations with the service representative. The goal always is to keep alive the personal-referral aspect of this business that has made it so successful. Enjoy your chat.

The reservation service representative will check the information you have provided in the host application and help you to set rates. Together, you will write a listing describing your B&B and detailing your house rules for the reservation service to use in material they publish about your place. They may also photograph your home so that the staff members who will be talking about it to travelers will be able to speak almost first-hand.

PREPARING YOUR LISTING

Your listing is a written description of your B&B. It should include the style of your home, what places of interest you are convenient to, a little about your family, details of the accommodations, and the rates. Any special features or restrictions should be included so that prospective guests can easily get a sense of what it will be like to visit your home. Here are some sample descriptions.

> **Host #17.** WALTON (New York, a rural location about 3 hours to New York City)—A chalet-style home on 200 beautiful acres with a large pond. A rowboat, pedal boat, and canoe are available. Fishing for rainbow trout, turkey hunting, and bow hunting. Host is retired but busy with gardening, making toys, and producing maple syrup. Hostess does tole painting, canes chairs, and makes quilts. Hostess will gladly baby-sit. This place is a nature lover's paradise. In December, guests can cut their own Christmas trees; and in spring, they can help sugar the maples. When snow is plentiful, guests can cross-country ski right on the property, then come inside to get warm in front

of the huge fireplace. The wooded area is a bird-watcher's delight, and the fall leaves are breathtaking. Hostess is a wonderful cook (from scratch) and enjoys using her imagination. This B&B is only 15 minutes from Delhi State College. Accommodations include: (a) large room with a double bed, three single beds, TV; (b) large room with a double bed, two single beds, one cot, TV. Guests share a bath. Smoking outside only. No pets. Children are welcome if well supervised (because of pond). Rates: Single $25, double $35 daily; single $150, double $210 weekly. Children under 2, free; extra persons in room, $10 each.

Host #362. MANHATTAN, GREENWICH VILLAGE (East 11 Street near Washington Square)—A fabulous decorator loft with high ceilings, bright colors, big windows, and designer baths. Your hostess is a French artist who also has her studio here. Accommodations include a room with king-size bed, private bath, and sunken tub. This apartment is available hosted most of the year, unhosted when the artist is abroad. Rates: Single $55, double $70 hosted. Unhosted $100 for two people, $125 for three people.

Host #244. KATONAH (1 hour from New York City)—A large stucco Mediterranean-style home set far back from the road on four beautifully landscaped acres near Caramoor and Harvey's School. This home is three minutes from Route 684 and the Saw Mill River Parkway. Host is a veterinarian who enjoys horseback riding. Hostess speaks Dutch and German, smokes, and enjoys gardening, sports, and sculpture. The family's four children are off at college and graduate school. Two dogs and two cats also live here. There is a newly built fifty-by-thirty-foot in-ground POOL. The accommodations include: (a) first-floor suite with queen-size bed, private bath with bidet, and family room with large-screen TV, fireplace, and terrace; (b) upstairs room with queen-size bed and private bath. Very deluxe, gourmet breakfast. Rates (a) $85 nightly, $500 weekly; (b) $65 nightly, $300 weekly.

Although your reservation service representative can write the description for you, your input will make it better. The important thing is to include enough to give the reader the right impression, yet be concise. Always make sure to include the size of the beds and type of bath. If you have a piano, pool, tennis courts, or any other special features, put them in capital letters so that a reader skimming for such items will notice them. This type of description will be needed for your service, directories, the Delta System, and your brochure, so take your time with it. Ask someone who writes well to edit it. If anything changes at your B&B, make sure to let your service know so that the change can be reflected in your listing.

THE HOST CONTRACT

Once you have been accepted by a reservation service, you will be asked to sign a host contract that spells out your legal responsibilities and those of your service. It should define your roles, indicate whether or not your approval is needed before bookings are made, and spell out commissions expected, the cancellation policy, host family responsibilities, guest responsibilities, telephone policy, rates, key policy, return bookings and referrals, and conditions for terminating the contract. Usually, written notice by either party is enough to cancel the contract, but commitments to take guests hold until the visit is past.

DAY-TO-DAY RELATIONS

In general, your reservation service is working every day to promote your B&B. A staff member will inform you that a particular guest is interested in staying with you and confirm that you are willing to accept this individual (and members of his or her party). If the reservation is for quite some time in the future, you may hear from the service by mail, but this is increasingly uncommon as B&B becomes better established.

Requests for reservations are considered pending by the service until a host accepts them. Guests are usually told to call back in a day or two to find out if the reservation has been approved by the host. At that time, a deposit is requested. At each stage until the check has been received and the confirmation sent out, the staff monitors the status of the reservation. It follows through on guests who fail either to call back after requesting a reservation or to send their deposit. Staff members know that it is very costly for a host to hold a reservation for someone who may not come. On rare occasions, especially during the busy season, an incomplete reservation can fall through the cracks because answering a ringing phone always takes priority over checking through files. If you are not certain that a reservation is definite, alert your service that you haven't received your confirmation. The staff will appreciate it.

Guests want to know fairly soon if their reservations have been confirmed, so much of the reservation service's business is done by telephone. You should let the service know the best times to contact you to save time and expense all around, and an answering machine is a must.

If you are going to be closed for a period of time for any reason, notify the service as far in advance as you can. You will not be penalized for taking breaks from hosting as you choose.

GET TO KNOW THE STAFF

The staff members are people that you should know personally. If you live close enough, stop by to introduce yourself. The better each person knows you and what type of B&B you have, the better he or she can represent your interests. Understand that there may be turnover. As new people come in, it behooves you to get to know them, too.

IN CASE OF EMERGENCY

Emergencies do happen once in a while. Guests understand that they are coming to a private home, and they are unlikely to want to visit a house that has become a full-fledged infirmary. In such cases, your service will try to find a substitute B&B for your guests, and you will forfeit any money received or promised for this booking. If they are touring and cannot be reached in time, the reservation service may ask you to direct them to the alternative B&B when they call you for directions. However, this would be highly unusual.

Cancellations on the part of the guests are also handled through the service. A statement of the cancellation policy should be included with the written confirmation notice sent to guests when reservations are made. Reservation services realize that you have gone to some expense and effort to freshen the guest rooms and made plans for or already purchased the food to serve for breakfast. Therefore, you and the service split the cancellation fee according to the normal commission percentage. If the fee for last-minute cancellation is one night's cost, you will get this amount minus your service's percentage. If you have already been paid for the stay by the reservation service, you will have to send the money back to the service so that it can send the guest the appropriate refund.

If a guest arrives and finds your place unacceptable because something is not as it should be (your pool is not functioning; your children have chicken pox), this is a cancellation for cause, and the guest's money will have to be refunded.

Sometimes the situation is not so clear. For example, one of my hostesses lives in a historic home with a small cottage on the property. She rents the cottage to year-round tenants but takes B&B guests in two beautiful bedrooms in the main house. The guests arrived Friday night and could not take a shower because there was no water. In the morning, there was still no water.

They liked the hostess but during breakfast said they had to leave because it was not acceptable that they had a private bath but no water. It turned out that the tenants had gone away for the weekend and left a toilet running. This was taking all the water from the old well system, leaving insufficient pressure in the line to get the water up to the second floor of the main house. The guests called our service and asked for a refund of the entire weekend because they had to make other, more costly, and inconvenient arrangements at the last minute. We felt they were justified and hoped to persuade them to try B&B another time, so we asked the hostess to return the full amount. This was a judgment; the service felt that the situation was one the hostess would have to resolve before we sent other guests. The hostess could have insisted on being paid for the night they stayed because they used the room and ate breakfast, but she agreed with us and refunded the money. When you work with a reservation service, such problems must be resolved as they arise. However, you must agree in principle to refund or not as the service sees fit; otherwise, the service will stop representing you.

Sometimes a guest's stay will be cut short by a family or work emergency. In these situations, the guest is expected to pay for one more night than he or she has stayed. For example, a guest who had to leave on the third day of a five-day stay would pay for four days and get one day's refund. If the guest is someone who stays with you often, you may prefer to give him a rain check for another visit. Offering a credit at the same B&B usually appeases an irate guest who claims not to have known about the cancellation policy or gives a host a way to offer something in lieu of refunding the additional nights. When a guest wants to use this credit, it must be at a time when the host has the room available. It is important to put a time limit on a credit so that it expires if not used within twelve months.

At special times of the year, certain places enforce no-refund policies with no exceptions. This is especially true of locales with one very active season or a few major events, such as college graduations or an annual festival.

Remember, the reservation service does double work for cancellations and loses money on them, too. The service does all it can to prevent them, but they are part of doing business with a growing clientele.

❖❖❖❖❖❖❖

Question: If the reservation service lists my B&B in its directory, won't that make my place open to the public?

Answer: No. The listings are never identified by name or street address. A reservation service's directory is usually available only by subscription or to those travelers who are members of the service. The only way anyone can contact your B&B is through your service. That contact sets in motion the screening and matching process that is the service's function. You benefit by having the attractions of your B&B (and your own interests) highlighted without having to leave promotional materials in public places. Of course, any errors or changes in your listing should be communicated to the service at once to avoid disappointments.

❖❖❖❖❖❖❖

Question: If I wanted to offer a special Singles Christmas next year, how should I go about having my reservation service promote this?

Answer: Write up a description of what you are offering. It should appear in service newsletters up to six months ahead of time to give guests a chance to make their holiday plans. Realize that this type of event is best done annually so that people who find out about it this year but can't attend can plan for next year. Here is a sample description written for just such a weekend.

A host in Ithaca, New York, is offering her home for a Singles Christmas. It begins Christmas Eve with a buffet supper and caroling by the piano or pump organ in front of the fire. Each guest is asked to bring a gift suitable for someone of either sex (value under $10). Gifts are opened on Christmas morning after a hearty breakfast. Then enjoy sports, games, or reading before Christmas dinner, which will be served with all the trimmings. A fix-it-yourself supper will be available from leftovers in the kitchen. Breakfast the next morning is included. The complete cost is $200 per person for two nights. Up to fourteen can be accommodated if people are willing to share rooms. The property is an 1865 farmhouse on 100 acres, ten minutes to Cornell and Ithaca College. Skate on Cayuga Lake. Ski Greek Peak or Song Mountain thirty minutes away. Two cats are in residence. To reserve, call Bed & Breakfast U.S.A., Ltd.

8

Operating Smoothly

You can keep B&B a rewarding experience for you and your guests by avoiding the most common pitfalls that can short-circuit a good time for all. Guests report dissatisfaction to reservation services when their reasonable expectations go unfulfilled in three basic ways:

- Confusion about arrival time and directions to the B&B

- Cleanliness of the bedroom, bath, or kitchen

- Advertised features that were not functional at the time of the visit

AVOID CONFUSION ABOUT ARRIVAL TIME AND DIRECTIONS

Once guests have paid for their accommodations and received written confirmation, it is up to them to let the host know what time to expect their party and to find out how to get there. Although guests know they are coming to a private home, many presume that the host will be there all day, just waiting for them to arrive. One suggestion for making sure your guests do call in advance is this: Don't routinely send out directions ahead of time. In this way, guests will have to contact you in order to find out exactly how to get to your home. Make it easy for guests to reach you by having an answering machine on when you don't want to take calls, and indicate in your recorded message that you want them to leave their number so that you can call back with directions. Do not record directions. Also, do not give your reservation service directions to mail out. Guests who already have printed directions are the ones who wait until they are five minutes away to call to let you know their arrival time.

Tips on Giving Directions

In giving directions, be exact. Go out and drive the route(s) into your town from the major thoroughfare(s), and write down the mileage for each portion of the drive. Remember, you are giving directions to people who are probably unfamiliar with your region, so give the simplest route rather than the fastest. Watch for landmarks a stranger might be able to identify at first glance, and mention them in your directions. Indicate when the guest may have traveled too far or made an incorrect turn at a difficult intersection. For example, if you get to the Taconic Parkway, you have gone too far. Drive the route both during the day and at night, and note any differences for the benefit of late-arriving travelers. Tell people where it's okay to park, and make sure your parking area and walkway are unobstructed and well lit.

Post a train or bus schedule near your business telephone so that you will be able to answer questions about service when guests call. Keep the numbers of the taxi and car rental companies there, too, and be able to give guests an idea of how far you are from the station and what the taxi fare should be.

Remember, if you are not home, another family member may answer the phone. So make sure that everyone is briefed on giving directions, answering questions, and making sure to get an approximate arrival time from the guests. Put the guests' name and arrival time on your calendar so that you will make sure someone is home to welcome them. Remind guests to phone in case of delay so that you will not be worried about them.

In major cities with good public transportation, guests may want to use it. Keep a transit map handy, and use the system yourself often enough to know the basics of getting to major attractions in town from your B&B.

Arrival Times

If your schedule is such that no one is home during the day, it is fine to set specific hours for arrival, but be sure to make it clear that it won't be possible for your guests to get into the house prior to this time. If you are delayed, or if the guest is late and you must leave to keep another commitment, you should have a standby system worked out with a neighbor so that someone will be on hand to greet the guest. Lateness should be rare if your directions are good and your guests are motivated to arrive at the agreed-on time.

Even in an unhosted B&B, someone is usually present to show the guest where things are and handle any financial business at the outset of the stay. Of course, if other members of your family are willing to do the greeting, the guest will not be left waiting, regardless of whether you have a cooperative neighbor. This is one situation you need to work out ahead of time with your family. When your guests arrive, you will also have to give them their key and explain your home's security system (if there is one). One kind of excitement that no one looks forward to is an uninformed guest mistakenly tripping an alarm and being mistaken by the police for an intruder.

PROVIDE CLEAN, ATTRACTIVE ACCOMMODATIONS

There are simple daily procedures for running your B&B that will keep things on an even keel no matter what your scale of operation. These are the very things that, if neglected, are sure to spoil the fun of your business. With B&B offering such enrichment and enjoyment, it makes sense to take timely care of those routine matters that mean so much to guests. You may find that you want help from other people to keep everything in ready-for-guests condition all the time, or you may find that maintaining your home in top condition is exactly what you like to do yourself because it brings you great pleasure to invest your time and personality in your B&B activities. Also, you may find that concentrating your attention on your home (if you have been accustomed to working away from home or haven't really looked at your home as a place of business in the past) leads you to follow pursuits that turn out to have a direct, positive impact on your business. Gardening; flower arranging; gourmet cooking; taking courses in interior design, woodworking, restoring antiques, or upholstering; or studying another language may become fringe benefits that make you a more versatile host and contribute to the beautification of your home.

Arriving guests expect to find a clean room with fresh sheets and towels, a fully equipped and sparkling bathroom, and clean and attractive public rooms and yard. In the vast majority of cases, your guests want to consider your B&B their home away from home and expect to do basic cleanup themselves, providing the articles to do so are at hand. Many hosts feel that for a stay of less than a week, there is no reason to enter the room at all until a guest has departed unless a guest room has special maintenance requirements such as a fireplace. Guests make their own beds (or not) as they see fit, take fresh towels and place used ones in the hamper or laundry room, and clean the tub and washbasin after they are finished in consideration of others who are also using the bathroom. All these are tasks most people would consider usual to do in their own homes. I personally empty wastebaskets daily, check to see if there are empty glasses or dishes to be brought down, and give the bathrooms a wipe-down whenever I pass by. I also check to make sure that there is soap in the dispenser, tissues in the tissue box, enough toilet tissue, and so forth.

To some extent, what guests expect is determined by how costly your accommodation is. If you are offering luxury accommodations in the $100-plus range, you will be expected to provide more extras and certainly do all daily maintenance yourself.

Another factor to be considered is how long the guests are to be with you. Guests who stay more than a week expect that you will clean their room, change the sheets and towels, and perhaps add some fresh flowers or a fruit basket (a nice thank-you for a lengthy booking). Cleaning includes both dusting and vacuuming. The guests should be told a day ahead of time that you will need to be in their room for an hour or two (enough time to wash the sheets and air the beds) in order to accomplish this. This will give the guests a chance to tidy up personal belongings and let you know what they might need.

We once had a couple come from overseas for the birth of their daughter's third child. They stayed three weeks and four days. We found them wonderfully amusing individuals and enjoyed their stay with us very much. On the second day, I popped my head into their room and saw a large suitcase propped open on my Victorian sofa. I told them that once they were unpacked, I would be happy to place their luggage in the attic so that they would have much more living space. Well, they lived out of that suitcase for their entire stay, never hanging anything in the closet or utilizing the dressers' considerable drawer space. Personal things were spread all over the marble-topped dressers, and even though I told them each week about my cleaning day. I was never able to clean off the furniture. Vacuuming and changing the linens were the best that could be done. These people, were on vacation and chose to live this way. Forcing them to be neat would have been an invasion of their privacy and would have made them feel uncomfortable. Sometimes, the best you can do is close the door and your eyes. Other guests are so neat that they make their beds even on the day they leave. You know that this is just what they do at home.

Always clean up and change sheets immediately after guests leave so that the room is ready for new guests. Do this even when you are not expecting new guests. Often on a Sunday after a houseful of weekenders have departed, I am tempted to leave the mess till Monday. It almost never fails that someone calls from within the community to discuss their daughter's upcoming wedding and to have a look at our rooms to see if they will want to place wedding guests here. The frantic race to get the house in order reminds me always to be company-ready.

LONG-TERM GUESTS

Eventually, you will get a request for a long-term guest—perhaps an executive on temporary assignment for three months, a teacher brought in to finish the school term for someone who is on leave, or a couple waiting for their house to be completed. Long-term guests often become part of your extended family. They will want laundry privileges, may help out with the dishes, walk the dog, baby-sit for your child, or barter some of their professional services for a reduction in room costs. Any experienced B&B host can recount numerous stories of antique clocks restored to working condition, family portraits photographed, a quilt made, or cooking lessons given in exchange for lodging. These very personal reminders of guests-become-friends are treasured long after the visit has ended. For many hosts, these encounters with other interesting and talented people are the major reason for their involvement with B&B.

CONTINUAL UPKEEP

If you have lived in your home for years, take a good look at it from the outside as well as the inside. What do you see as you drive up the street? Does your house need a new coat of paint? Are your bushes overgrown? What impression will your guests get as they follow your directions to the parking area and step inside your home? Remember that you are trying to get some distance from your personal perspective and see your home as a stranger would. Day-to-day cleaning and making breakfast never stop, but certain routine maintenance or freshening up must be done seasonally or as needed. Pretend that you have just bought your home. Evaluate what needs to be done to bring its general condition up to snuff.

Saving on Maintenance

When we moved to our home in Croton-on-Hudson, B&B was part of our strategy to make living in our dream house a reality. We had an energy audit, insulated our attic floor, put storm windows on our sun porch, and installed insulated draperies. My husband is good with his hands, and between us we can take on many of the projects that others hire professionals to do. Saving on the cost of outside labor is tremendously helpful to our budget, but projects take longer because they have to be completed on weekends and in the evenings. Needless to say, you have to enjoy the work as well as the results and have a great deal of commitment and determination to keep up the momentum. We found that it was necessary to work on a project for no longer than three months at a time and then take at least a month off before doing anything else on the house. Schedule vacations and times when you have no house responsibilities to give you a breather and renew your strength before tackling a new project.

We began by making a list of maintenance jobs such as cleaning the gutters, caring for the lawn, and draining the radiators. Then we decided which chores we would hire help for. We decided lawn care was more efficiently done by a gardener, leaving us free to tackle the jobs where very skilled labor would cost us dearly. We put regular tasks onto our calendar so that they wouldn't get lost in the shuffle.

Then came the list of special projects. It is always necessary to start by making a list of the projects you want to complete, estimating their cost and the time needed to complete them, and setting priorities. Remember, best estimates for cost and time are usually wrong but nonetheless help you to make plans and execute them.

Once the work is completed, your home will require constant maintenance. Paint needs to be touched up; sheets need to be replaced before they become frayed or shabby.

Before you open your B&B, your public rooms should be finished, the outside of your home should be appealing and well maintained, and the guest rooms should look warm and inviting. If your goal is to fix up three rooms for guests, it may be wise to start with one. Then, as your business grows and you get the feel of this way of life, you can finish additional rooms. Some of the hosts I have met have photographed their homes during restoration and transition and keep this album both for their own enjoyment and sense of accomplishment and to show to interested guests. Many guests are in the process of restoring their own homes and enjoy exchanging solutions to problems encountered along the way. Don't, however, assume that all guests want a blow-by-blow description of everything you have done.

DECORATING OR REDECORATING

Like maintenance, decorating or redecorating your house to make it a more attractive B&B is an ongoing process. In choosing a decorating style, turn again to your reservation service for guidelines about what travelers in your region expect. Within the boundaries of what qualifies any room as a standard accommodation, you should aim for something distinctive that reflects your own personality and interests or something unique about your home or area. Emphasize comfort and convenience, the former for your guest's benefit, the latter for yours. If you have a collection of something lovely, the guest room may be the place to display it. If you are interested in upgrading a simple room into a higher category, review the characteristics of an executive accommodation, on page 44, and spend your money on those features that will return your investment sooner, such as a small private bath, a set of sliding doors to a small patio, a pullman kitchenette across one end of the room, a sauna or hot tub. The room may need something as simple as new bed-spreads and curtains or something as elaborate as a complete architectural renovation. The hosts I know run the gamut from people who just added a few items to their ordinary rooms to those who purchased faded mansions and restored them to resplendent condition specifically to open a B&B. (For some of their stories, see Chapter 10, "Interviews with Successful Hosts.")

Examples of decor in a typical B&B.

Garage Saling or I Can't Believe
I Filled the Whole House!

I would like to share with you the tips that I followed in finding the treasures that make guests ask me if my family has lived here for generations:

A seven-foot couch for $100, a carved Victorian dresser for $25, a service of fine china for ten for $150—these are just a few of the things I have found at garage and estate sales. You, too, if you have some weekend mornings to spare, a list of your furniture needs, and an adventurous spirit that enjoys the thrill of the hunt, can acquire many one-of-a-kind items at a fraction of their retail prices to make your B&B very special, indeed. Here are a few tips, the results of many an enjoyable weekend.

155

1. Shop in the best neighborhoods. Get a good map, and use it to explore expensive areas. People with a lot of money often don't know the value of what they have to sell. They will often price things according to whether or not they like them.

2. Favor places that are run by the owners rather than professional salespeople. Professionals hike the price by 25 percent. But it is also worth getting to know the professionals because they can look out for certain things that you've had trouble finding.

3. Set limits for yourself in advance so that you will know if something is in your range and won't be tempted to overspend. This is especially important for auctions.

4. Certain things are easy to reupholster using a staple gun; others need professional attention. It is wise to know the retail cost of a new piece of furniture and what reupholstery costs before you bring home a bargain sofa and find you need to spend $1,000 plus fabric to re-upholster it.

5. Take some risks. For example, if you think that no one else will want or have a place for some item, submit a low bid (a final offer that you will pay), and ask the owner or salesperson to call you after the sale if it is still available and he or she is interested in selling at your price. Sometimes this gets you a real bargain.

6. If you don't see what you are looking for, ask. Some-times this will remind the seller of a piece that was too awkward to bring downstairs.

7. Sellers seldom expect to get their asking price. Don't be afraid to offer less and negotiate.

8. Dealers try to get there early. If you are serious, emulate

them. They can't afford to pay what you can because they have to mark up the items for resale.

9. Garage sales are not consistent. Realize that you often go to ten bad ones for every terrific one. When you find yourself at a bad one, just count that as one step in your quest. As in any treasure hunt, there are many detours and dead ends on the way to the trove.

Good luck!

HANDLING SPECIAL FEATURES OF YOUR B&B

You will probably include certain special features of your home in your B&B description. If you do, guests will expect to have access to them. Therefore, if something prevents the use of a special attraction, it is very important that guests be told about the problem in advance. Understand that they may choose to make other plans, in which case you will owe them a complete refund because cancellation policies do not apply when a host home cannot offer what it claims to. If an attraction is seasonal—for example, your swimming pool—make sure to specify when it is open. Guests visiting during a hot Indian summer weekend in late September may be disappointed to find your pool closed on Labor Day. It will protect you to be able to show that the Labor Day closing date is listed in your printed description.

Of course, use of special features may require special rules for guests, rules that you are responsible for telling them as well as posting for consultation if you are not at home. Do not assume that guests will know how to use your facilities. Special instructions will be required for use of your fireplace, pool, hot tub, sauna, spa, weight training equipment, sound system, VCR, laundry facilities, microwave, office machinery, and the like.

A welcoming letter in each guest room letting guests know which facilities in your house are available for their use and if there are any limitations or special precautions that must be taken is very useful and will be appreciated. Because every B&B is different, what you will include in your letter may be very different from what I put in mine. A farm B&B might need to give a map showing the walk down to the paddock to meet the horses and tips about which horses like apples and how to offer the apple with the hand open, so the horse takes only the apple, not a nibble of fingers, too. You might set a one-apple limit for each horse so your guests don't overfeed them while trying to be nice.

A host with a VCR and a collection of old movies will want to provide instruction for using the machinery as well as how the films are arranged. Directions and the phone number of a nearby video store might be included so that guests can take advantage of a rainy afternoon to relax and catch a film they have wanted to see.

Fireplaces

The romance of a crackling fire on a cold night is an unbeatable attraction for many getaway-weekend guests. If your fireplace is in a public room, arrange for it to be laid ready to start, and let your guests know how to fully open the flue and light the fire. If guests are arriving in the evening, it is very welcoming and cozy to greet them in front of a toasty fire.

If the fireplace is in the guest room, assume your guests will want to use it. Lay the first fire yourself, and leave extra wood close enough so that guests can keep it going without disturbing their privacy or yours. Leave a written reminder on the mantelpiece about when to close the flue, and inquire about it when you meet the guest for breakfast, too. Show guests where the fire extinguisher is located (preferably in the guest closet). Ask them to call you immediately if there's the slightest problem with the flue or any other aspect of the fireplace (such as, screen not closing properly or smoke in the room). If guests are staying more than a day or two, show them how to clean out the ashes, or ask them to let you know when you can go into the room to take care of it. Ashes can impair the draw of your fireplace if the buildup is considerable, and their smell can permeate the entire house very quickly.

Pool Safety

As long a you have a private-home B&B, not under special state or commercial regulations, you usually do not need a lifeguard at your pool. Check your state and local regulations. If there is no lifeguard, it is up to you to ensure safety at poolside by establishing rules and providing life preservers and life jackets for young children and nonswimmers. It would be wise for someone in your family to know cardiopulmonary resuscitation (CPR), lifesaving, and how to give mouth-to-mouth resuscitation. Any course you take will be both practical and tax deductible.

During the swimming season, establish a routine for testing the pool water and adding chemicals to it. Try to do this at a time when few people would want to swim. Let parents know that children are not allowed at poolside without a responsible adult present. Make sure any nonswimming child wears a life jacket at poolside, even if the youngster is not planning to go in the water. Make sure anything served near the pool is served on plastic plates or in plastic glasses. Glass can shatter by a pool, and even though you sweep up carefully, a stray piece of glass could become lodged in someone's foot.

Keep a first aid kit handy and an extra bottle of suntan lotion in case guests forget theirs. It's very thoughtful to have some sun-block lotion, especially for babies, and make sure that there are some shady umbrellas for adults to sit under while they supervise the children.

Most locales have rules about fencing around a pool. Few, though, have rules about pool covers. Make sure that your pool is safe in the winter as well as summer by having a safety cover and keeping your gate closed and telling parents that no one is allowed near the pool when it is closed.

Laundry Facilities

Even guests who stay only a day or two may need to wash out something. Guests who stay longer will need access to a washer and dryer. It makes it very comfortable for guests if the hosts provides information about what they are free to use. If guests are sharing a bath, it would be embarrasing to hang stockings or undergarments over the tub to dry. Let guests know that they can hang up a few articles in your laundry room, or offer to include some of their things with the family wash.

I have instructions posted next to my washer and dryer, but I try to be there the first time guests use the machine so that I can answer questions and make sure they understand how to clean the filters. Because I do so much laundry on a routine basis, I make sure guests understand that household laundry has priority. In the case of long-term guests, I expect them to purchase their own laundry soap and bleach; otherwise, I do not. I keep the iron and ironing board in the extra linen closet on the guest room level of the house and happily set it up for guests who need it.

Other hosts set up their laundry rules differently. A hostess who has a number of relocating executives as long-term guests does their laundry and is paid extra for the service. How you handle laundry is up to you. The important thing is to realize that many guests have laundry needs and that you should be the one to initiate the discussion. The last thing you want is for a guest to wash out undergarments and hang them to dry on your antique wooden headboard.

MAINTAINING YOUR SATISFACTION

Hosts become dissatisfied when guests' expectations are unreasonable. Most commonly, this happens when guests fail to sense the line between the kind of service they can demand in a hotel and the attention to which they are entitled in a private-home B&B. In general, the more expensive your accommodation, the more hotel-type service people tend to expect. Even when you do not bill yourself as a luxury B&B, you may find yourself being asked to cross this line.

Setting Limits

Along with making guests aware of what they may do, it is always necessary to make any limits clear. For instance, if you permit smoking but restrict it to certain parts of your home, these limits must be spelled out. In addition to including this information in any literature about your B&B, you will want to be very clear about it in your welcome letter. You may want to mention your breakfast hours, how much notice is required for candlelight dinners, or anything else that a guest needs to know.

Telephone Use

One potentially troublesome issue is that of the telephone. It is in your best interest to think through your telephone policy and spell it out. Almost every guest will at some time need to make or receive calls. Very few B&B's have or want to install a pay phone. In addition to being commercial, they are very expensive and don't pay for themselves with only limited use. You may want to have two lines, one for incoming calls (the number you give out) and the other for outgoing use. Regardless of whether you have one or two lines, it is important for guests to know that they can receive calls at your home and make emergency calls and short local calls to restaurants, theaters, and the like. Any long-distance calls to check on the children at home or whatever should be charged to the guest's home phone or paid for with a credit card. Most business travelers are used to this. Occasionally, long-term guests will keep a running total of their long-distance calls and pay you as the bills come in. This is sometimes a nuisance but seldom causes real problems. What does cause problems is a guest tying up your phone for hours, making it difficult for you to make or receive calls. So remember, get phone policy straight at the outset.

There should be a pad of paper by the phone with a pen or pencil tied to it (so that it won't walk away). Any message taken by anyone at the house should be dated (including time of call) and should indicate who the message is for, who it is from, and the number to be called. There should be a standard place where messages for family members are put. Messages for guests should be left in their rooms.

YOUR HOME OFFICE

Whether your home office is an entire room or just a desk in the corner of your family room, it should be the one place where you keep all your business-related things. It should include:

- Your guest book.

- Receipts and guest contracts.

- Checkbook specifically for this business. Keep your personal account separate so that you can keep good track of your B&B expenses and income.

- Sales tax form folder.

- Envelope or cashbox for receipts for business expenses.

- Manila envelopes for reservation information and other communications with your reservation service (saves extra telephone calls).

- A calendar to mark the dates you are booked, the number of people in each party, and which rooms they will be staying in.

- Business cards.

- Business stationery for letters to guests or media.

- Correspondence notes with business logo or name for short notes to upcoming guests or thank-yous to others who help you with your business.

- Christmas cards or other holiday cards to send to former guests.

- Postage scale and stamps.

- Telephone answering machine.

- Scratch pads, pens, pencils, tape, eraser, mailing labels, scissors, and stapler.

- Typewriter (makes correspondence look professional when you enclose a cover letter with your press kit). But avoid typing personal notes to guests; a handwritten note is a nice touch in these days of electronic everything.

- Home computer for financial record keeping, recipe storage, and so on.

- Floppy disks and software.

- Books, periodicals, course outlines and notes, dealing with running a B&B or small business in general. A set of reference cookbooks is also a good idea to help you enliven your breakfasts.

THE RARITY: A TROUBLESOME GUEST

If you accept only guests who have been screened by your reservation service and have prepaid for their stay, most of them will cause you no problems. But on rare occasions, you will have a troublesome guest. When this happens, you must evaluate the problem. A guest whose personality is not to your liking but who is not disruptive to your home or interfering with the enjoyment of other guests is just someone who will be there a short time and then easily forgotten. If a guest disrupts your home or interferes with the enjoyment of other guests, you must handle the situation immediately. Take the guest aside, and speak to him or her about why what they are doing is disruptive. If necessary, ask this guest to stay somewhere else. It is up to you under these circumstances to determine whether it is appropriate to refund the payment for the balance of the stay. Certainly, if a guest is violating house rules by smoking or has smuggled in a pet, you are under no obligation to refund anything. If guests have become intoxicated, are having a loud argument with each other, and have awakened other guests, ask them to quiet down. Under no circumstances should you get involved with a drunken, hostile person. In such a case, wait until morning, and ask the guest to leave. Rest assured, however, that most hosts have never had occasion to do this.

SEPARATING HOME FROM WORK

Burnout is common in service businesses when people become too involved in their businesses. It is important when you work at home to make time for privacy, family activities, and visiting with personal friends. Sometimes, especially during your busy season, the outside stimulation of meeting so many interesting people may make you forget to maintain your relationships with friends and the community. Don't allow this to happen to you. Schedule vacations. Plan activities out of the house, and enjoy them. Although you may become very involved in your B&B-related activities and in being a pioneer in a new industry, don't let B&B become the only thing you talk about. Remember, the most successful hosts are interesting to guests because they lead rich and exciting lives.

❖❖❖❖❖❖❖

Question: What about house rules for pets? Our two dogs are pretty accepting of others, and we have a fenced-in area for them. They sleep outside in a dog house except on the coldest winter nights, when we put them on a screened-in porch. Our town strictly enforces a leash law; the first offense costs the owner $25, the second is $50, and every one after that goes up to $100, plus the costs of having the animal boarded at the local police station impoundment area ($15 a day). Also, there is a local ordinance requiring owners to clean up streets, sidewalks, and green spaces after their pets. Will I be responsible for pets of guests staying with me? What if a visiting pet damages furnishings in my home or, worse yet, damages a neighbor's garden or menaces a child? I know my dogs very well and have spent a great deal of time training them well. How can I be sure visiting pets will behave? Am I responsible for providing pet food?

Answer: If you want to take pets, you will have a large clientele. Consult with your attorney and insurance company about correct clauses to put in your guest contract covering the situations that you have mentioned. Accepting pets will probably increase your potential liability. Have a frank discussion with the owner before the pet arrives. The guest may decide that the regulations will interfere with other plans for the visit and chose instead to board the animal or hire a sitter to care for it at home. Ask about the animal's training. It is wisest for owners to bring their animal's customary food along rather

than switch its diet on a trip. Guests need to know that they
are fully responsible for seeing to the care of the pet unless you
arrange otherwise in advance.

Establish a relationship with a good veterinarian in your
area in case a pet should fall ill during its stay with you. Think
carefully about where you will allow the guest to bring the pet
on your premises, and tell the guests exactly what you allow.
Many people traveling with pets fully expect that the animal
will be allowed to sleep in the guest's bedroom, perhaps in the
bed. Many people with pets allow them the full run of their
own homes and do not realize that others would never dream
of allowing a cat on the beds or upholstered furniture.

Finally, realize that other guests will be coming during
the same period. If they have allergies and have chosen your
B&B because you have no cats of your own and you allow a cat
to come, it may spoil their whole vacation. Remember, you
have agreed to provide for the comfortable hospitality of all
your guests.

For these reasons, most hosts, even true pet lovers, seldom permit guests' pets.

9

Best Breakfasts

For B&B guests, the best breakfasts are those that suit their schedules and give them a chance to get to know their hosts a little better. Obviously, weekdays, when everyone is trying to get out to take care of the day's business, require one approach, and lazy Sundays on the terrace, with everyone in a relaxed and expansive mood, require another. So, your breakfast style will vary depending on who the guests are, what their food preferences are, how much time you have to share, and how much fun you get out of food preparation. For many hosts, providing a unique breakfast is a real high point of a visit, for others, the simpler, the better.

If you aspire to running a deluxe B&B, excellent food beautifully served is an integral part of what you need to plan for every time you have guests. If you have a garden, no ingredients can surpass what is truly fresh and ripe. This chapter gives sample recipes and includes a list of cookbooks to explore when you feel yourself falling into a beginning-of-the-day rut.

Are your guests tired of cereal out of the box? Unable to face another road stand name-brand doughnut? Then they're ready for your best breakfasts!

WHEN TO SERVE BREAKFAST

Whether you have rigid breakfast hours or a flexible schedule according to your guests needs should be determined by your life-style. Discuss the options with your family. Some hosts who have many outside demands on their time opt for fixed breakfast hours: 7:00 to 8:00 A.M. or 9:00 A.M. on weekdays and 8:00 to 10:00 A.M. or 9:00 to 11:00 A.M. on weekends. This is a way to limit the time expected of you in the kitchen. Make sure to include these breakfast hours in any written material you prepare or in a guest's confirmation notice. If you decide to be flexible, it is necessary to touch base with your guests each night before so that you will know what time to have breakfast ready the next morning.

PLANNING AHEAD

In planning your menu, first take into consideration how many guests you will serve. Serving a romantic breakfast for two guests and serving to a family of five who will shortly be followed at your table by two adult couples require different planning. You have spoken to your guests the night before, so you have a good idea whether they will be in a hurry or ready for a leisurely breakfast of something special.

In Europe, a continental breakfast of a croissant and coffee is the rule. Not so in America. Most guests really look forward to this first and most important meal of the day.

PRESENTATION

Sometimes, guests arrive at the table at different times. In such cases, it is easier to serve a buffet-style meal. That way, guests can help themselves and take a seat at the table. Whether you serve buffet-style or serve each guest once he or she is seated, follow the same basics of setting a pretty table: an attractive centerpiece or floral arrangement (seasonal changes add interest; silk flowers are sensible in winter), spotless glassware and silver, candles (collect an assortment of holders), cloth napkins, tablecloths or place mats, and napkin rings. Some hosts collect table accents of all types (from butter molds to interesting vases, vintage dishes and cutlery, or curio salt and pepper shakers) to make each day's breakfast setting different. Others assemble vintage linens to create exceptionally nostalgic settings for special occasions. And remember, all such acquisitions used for B&B are tax deductible.

Breakfast in bed, if you offer it, should be served on lovely trays with fine china, crystal, a fresh flower, cloth napkins, piping-hot coffee, and wonderful food. A morning paper is a nice extra.

TIME SAVING TIPS

1. Learn to make the best use of your freezer and microwave. (If you don't have a microwave, plan to purchase one. It's a true time-saver for your B&B needs.)

2. Whenever you bake, prepare a double batch, and freeze the extras. (Always mark the date and item description on the wrapper so that you will use the food while it is still good.)

3. Arrange fresh berries on cookie sheets and freeze them whole; then bag them to enjoy when the season is past—in pancakes and mixed into fruit cups and fillings.

4. Wrap things individually for the freezer so that you can prepare enough for one guest or several without thawing more than you need.

5. Don't feel locked into classic breakfast food. Freeze cooked chicken to use as a filling for crepes, cooked beans for Mexican burritos or a pot of thick soup or chili for skiers who may need a heartier breakfast.

6. As you use up the last of the orange juice, make more. If

your pitcher is always full, you won't have to keep guests waiting while you make more.

7. There are many coffee makers with timers that allow you to prepare the pot the night before and set it to go on before you get to the kitchen. Another advantage to having the coffee ready early is that often a guest will awaken very early and wander into the kitchen. It is nice to find coffee waiting.

8. If breakfast is to be served early, you may also want to set the table the night before.

OTHER TIPS

1. Keep your kitchen clean, even when cooking. Don't let garbage accumulate. Throw away eggshells and plastic wrap instead of leaving them on the counter.

2. Try to incorporate some regional specialties in your menus, but have some standby alternatives in case not all your guests are adventurous eaters. For example, most people enjoy their first taste of real maple syrup, but not everyone can survive Mexican hot chilis.

3. Do most of your breakfast preparation before the guests get to the table so that you will be able to join them if that is appropriate. Make sure the condiments are on the table. You will of course have to go back into the kitchen to take away the first course and bring in the second or get more coffee, but you should still be the gracious host. And it should look easy. Don't give the appearance of being a jack-in-the-box.

4. Most guests enjoy it when you join them at the table. They like the personal attention and the chance to ask questions about the region, restaurants, local events

and places of interest, and so on. Whether you dine with them, chat, or just serve is your decision. Keep in mind that a romantic couple or four friends who haven't seen each other in a long time may have little interest in getting to know you better. In such cases, it is best for you to give them their privacy.

5. Don't start clearing the table the minute your guests have finished their last mouthful. Often, they will enjoy relaxing and getting to know each other better over another cup of coffee. Once you start to take dirty dishes away, it may be perceived as a signal that breakfast is over and that you are anxious for them to leave.

SPECIAL GUESTS

Children

Most children will be less than excited by the opportunity to sample your breakfast specialties. Consequently, it is a good idea to have your pantry well stocked with breakfast cereals, juice, milk, and peanut butter (if all else fails). Have a high chair and bib available if you accept little ones. A supply of plastic plates, bowls, and cups will serve you well. The ones with famous cartoon characters painted on them are especially well received by youngsters, and your fine china and stoneware will be protected. Speak to the parents about the child's tastes before planning to serve your gourmet offering for him or her. If there is more than one child present (even if they are from different parties), they are often much happier to be served on a little table of their own near the TV. Saturday morning cartoons are likely to be preferable to the sophisticated conversation of adults trying to get to know each other. However, before you separate parents and children, speak the the parents so that they don't feel you are trying to exclude the child.

Vegetarians

Vegetarians are usually quite easy to plan for because most eat eggs, and French toast or pancakes are enjoyed by everyone. If they don't eat eggs, try yogurt, fresh breads, and jams. If you are a vegetarian, include this information in any description of your B&B so that the lack of meat won't be a surprise.

Health Problems

Whether your guests have health problems or are just concerned with preventing them, many people today prefer to avoid fat, sugar, salt, or caffeine. Stock up on decaffeinated coffee and teas. Herbal teas may or may not be caffeine-free, so read the label. It is usually not too difficult to plan menus around these requirements. You can easily offer an alternative to someone who has a restricted diet and still serve your main breakfast selection to the rest of your guests. People with severe allergies may bring their own food. Don't be insulted; be thankful, and do your best to serve it as attractively as possible.

Kosher Food

If your guests keep a kosher kitchen at their home, they may not be able to eat breakfast at your home. Keeping a kosher kitchen is a way of life, not something you can do for a weekend to accommodate a particular set of guests. In such cases, it is best to ask what (if anything) they can eat and whether they would prefer to be served on paper plates if your dishes are not kosher. They may choose to bring their own food or not eat. Again, don't be insulted. However, if you keep a kosher kitchen, make sure to mention this in any material about your B&B. You will of course be able to offer an array of wonderful foods, but because there are certain limitations, it is best for guests to know in advance.

WIDEN YOUR CULINARY HORIZONS

Develop the habit of browsing through cookbooks for new ideas. Recipes in books from major publishers are kitchen-tested, so you will waste less time (and ingredients) on recipes that fail. Try out new recipes on your family before offering them to guests. Here is a list of cookbooks dedicated to the first meal of the day; they will give you a sense of the vast array of recipes from which to choose. You may also find wonderful things in more comprehensive books.

Durand, Pauline W., and Yolande Languirand. *Brunch: Great Ideas for Planning, Cooking, and Serving.* New York: Barron, 1978.

Janericco, Terence. *The Book of Great Breakfasts and Brunches.* New York: Van Nostrand Reinhold, 1983.

Jester, Pat. *Brunch Cookery.* New York: Dell, 1981.

Phillips, Jill M. *The Good Morning Cook Book.* New York: Pelican, 1976.

The following books emphasize entertaining and use of specialized food groups.

Gorman, Marion. *Cooking with Fruit.* Emmaus, Penn.: Rodale Press, 1983.

London, Sheryl, and Mel London. *The Herb and Spice Cookbook.* Emmaus, Penn.: Rodale Press, 1986.

Sass, Lorna, J. *Christmas Feasts from History.* New York: Metropolitan Museum of Art and Irena Chalmers Cookbooks, 1981.

SAMPLE MENUS

An asterisk (*) indicates that the recipe is included in this chapter.

❖❖❖❖❖❖

HONEYMOON BREAKFAST ON A YACHT

Strawberry Gateau Des Crepes*
Whipped Cream
Champagne

❖❖❖❖❖❖

BUSINESSWOMAN'S BREAKFAST WHILE OVERLOOKING THE HUDSON

Baked Apples or Pears in Crust*
Home-baked Biscuits*
Van Wyck Baked Eggs*

❖❖❖❖❖❖

BREAKFAST BEFORE VISITING THE ZOO WITH CHILDREN

Orange Juice
Phyllo Blintzes*
Assorted Jams
Egg and Cheese Casserole with Herbs*

❖❖❖❖❖❖

BREAKFAST PICNIC ON VENICE BEACH

Bran mixed cereal,* Barbara's mixed cereal,* Meusli*
Fruit Curry*
Yogurt

❖❖❖❖❖❖

FIFTH AVENUE APARTMENT BREAKFAST WITH SUNDAY TIMES

Lox and Bagels
Capers, Cream Cheese, Raw Onion, Tomatoes
Vegetable Zip*

174

❖❖❖❖❖❖❖

10-BELOW SKI BREAKFAST

Roasted Pancakes*
Peach Topping*
Canadian Bacon
Hot Chocolate

❖❖❖❖❖❖❖

PREAKNESS BRUNCH WITH A GREEK ACCENT

Lemon Soup*
Trigona*
Shrimp Paste*
Lemon Sauce*
Yogurt Sauce*
Greek Olives

❖❖❖❖❖❖❖

COLLEGE INTERVIEW BREAKFAST

Raspberry Shake*
Shredded Wheat Bread*
Coddled Egg*

❖❖❖❖❖❖❖

CLASS REUNION BRUNCH

Confetti*
Novelty Breads and Rolls
(Chapati, Poppy-seed Rolls, Rye Crescent Rolls, Potato Bread,
Whole Wheat–Sunflower Seed Bread, Croutons)*
Welsh Rarebit*
Rhubarb Fizz*

❖❖❖❖❖❖❖

BREAKFAST BEFORE HOLIDAY SHOPPING

Grapefruit-avocado Cup*
Egg Burritos* or Cheese Strata*
Coffee

❖❖❖❖❖❖❖

SINGLES WEEKEND OMELET BREAKFAST

Assorted Muffins
Omelets by the Dozen*
Green Tea

❖❖❖❖❖❖❖

HEARTY WINTER BREAKFAST

Apple Tart*
Homemade Sausages*
Green Tomato Pie*

❖❖❖❖❖❖❖

RECIPE TREASURY

STRAWBERRY GATEAU DES CREPES (Serves 2)

6 small vanilla crepes
2 cups whole strawberries
2 cups strawberries, slightly mashed and sweetened to taste
Strawberry jam
1 cup confectioners' sugar
Shredded coconut

Place each crepe on a decorative individual serving plate. Spread small amount of jam on crepe; then spoon on sweetened mashed strawberries. Repeat this process twice. Arrange whole strawberries around edge of gateau. Sprinkle with confectioners' sugar and shredded coconut. Serve with whipped cream.

❖❖❖❖❖❖❖

VANILLA CREPES (Makes 32 to 35 crepes)

3 eggs
½ teaspoon salt
1½ cups flour
2 cups milk
1 tablespoon sugar
2 teaspoons vanilla extract
2 tablespoons melted butter

In blender combine eggs, flour, milk, salt, sugar, and vanilla. Blend on low for a minute. Scrape batter down sides with rubber spatula. Add melted butter and blend again for fifteen seconds. Refrigerate for at least 1 hour. Stir batter before cooking. Cook on upside-down crepe griddle or in traditional pan.

Once made, crepes can be stored 2 to 3 days in the refrigerator, if wrapped tightly in foil or plastic bags. They will store in the freezer for up to four months sealed in freezer bags. Thaw them before trying to separate them. Putting a sheet of waxed paper between each crepe before freezing makes them easier to separate when you are ready to use them. Heat in microwave oven before filling.

❖❖❖❖❖❖❖

BAKED APPLES OR PEARS IN CRUST

Small apples or pears, one for each person
1 piecrust for every three apples or pears (Ready-made crusts available in refrigerated department of supermarket work fine.)
Raisins and raspberry jam mixed together (Or substitute a variety of other sweet fillings.)
Granulated sugar

Core each apple or pear from the top. Do not go all the way through, but carve out a pocket 1 inch across. Spoon filling into pocket. Cut piecrust into four quarters. Cover with quarter of piecrust rolled thin. Use a little extra from fourth quarter of crust to fill in any gaps. Make a simulated stem; if you want to be fancy, add a pastry leaf as well. Sprinkle with sugar. Bake in preheated 375-degree oven for 30 minutes or until golden brown.

177

❖❖❖❖❖❖❖

HOME-BAKED BISCUITS (Serves 4 to 6)

1 ¾ cups unbleached flour
¼ cup soy flour
1 tablespoon baking powder
½ teaspoon salt
⅞ cup heavy cream
½ tablespoon honey
⅓ cup butter or margarine, melted

In a medium bowl, combine dry ingredients. Add cream and honey, stirring only until dough forms a ball. Knead for 1 minute on a lightly floured surface. Roll dough out to ½-inch to ¾-inch thickness. Cut into round biscuits approximately 2 inches in diameter. Dip each biscuit in melted butter before placing it on a greased cookie sheet. Bake in middle of preheated 450-degree oven for 10 to 12 minutes or until golden brown. Serve at once.

Variations

Here are a few suggestions for extraflavorful biscuits. Just stir in listed ingredients before adding liquids. For bite-size party appetizers, roll dough to the same thickness to fit a straight-sided baking pan. Cut to desired size after cooling for 5 minutes, but still serve warm.

with Cheddar and Bacon *Add ½ cup grated cheddar cheese and ¼ cup bacon bits.*

with Chives *Add 2 tablespoons chives.*

with Curry *Add 3 tablespoons curry powder.*

with Herbs *Add 1 tablespoon of your favorite dry herb, such as sage, savory, tarragon, or thyme.*

with Garlic *Add 2 tablespoons very finely minced garlic.*

with Onion *Add 3 tablespoons very finely minced onion, ⅛ teaspoon pepper, and ½ teaspoon caraway seeds.*

with Parsley *Add 4 tablespoons minced fresh parsley.*

with Stuffed Olives *Add 3 tablespoons finely minced green olives stuffed with pimento.*

❖❖❖❖❖❖❖

VAN WYCK BAKED EGGS (Serves 1)

2 eggs
Italian seasoned bread crumbs
1½ strips bacon, cooked until crisp and drained
1 tablespoon cottage cheese
½ slice Swiss cheese
1½ tablespoons Cheddar cheese, crumbled
½ fresh cherry tomato
1 sprig fresh parsley or other fresh herb
Vegetable cooking spray

Spray vegetable cooking spray into an individual cassolette. Coat sides and bottom of cassolette with seasoned bread crumbs. Break bacon into bits and place in bottom of cassolette. Gently break both eggs over bacon bits. Place cottage cheese on top of eggs. Cover with Swiss and Cheddar cheeses. Garnish with cherry tomato half. (Do not substitute any other variety of tomato because they will run.) Bake in preheated 350-degree oven for 30 minutes. Serve with fresh parsley garnish or a sprinkling of fresh herbs. You can prepare a number of these eggs at once and pop them into the oven half an hour before you expect each guest for breakfast.

❖❖❖❖❖❖❖

PHYLLO BLINTZES (Serves 8 to 10)

1 pound phyllo pastry
½ pound butter, melted
2 cups ricotta cheese
1 egg
Pinch of salt
¼ teaspoon vanilla extract
2 tablespoons sugar
1 tablespoon melted butter

Thaw phyllo according to the directions on package. Mix ingredients for filling with a spoon until smooth. Take 2 sheets of phyllo dough, and lightly brush top sheet with butter. Cut sheets into 4 long strips. Place 1 tablespoon of filling on bottom of each strip. Fold corner of phyllo over filling; then fold like a flag, alternating left to right to shape a triangle. Place seam down on buttered cookie sheet and brush again with butter. The blintzes can be baked at once or frozen for later use.

Bake at 375 degrees for 20 minutes or until golden brown. If you turn the oven off and open the door slightly, the blintzes will hold for up to a half hour. Serve with preserves.

Thaw frozen blintzes overnight in refrigerator. Before baking them, brush them again with melted butter. Bake in a 250-degree oven for 15 minutes. (Heating them in the microwave makes them soggy.)

EGG AND CHEESE CASSEROLE WITH HERBS (Serves 4 to 6)

8 eggs
½ cup milk
½ cup cottage cheese or ricotta
2 slices Swiss cheese, torn into small pieces
2 tablespoons of your favorite herb (such as chives, oregano, dill)
½ cup crumbled Cheddar cheese
Vegetable cooking spray

Whip eggs and milk with a wire wisk. Add cottage cheese, Swiss cheese, and herbs, and mix with wooden spoon. Pour into a deep pie dish sprayed with vegetable cooking spray. Sprinkle with crumbled Cheddar. Bake at 375 degrees for 45 minutes to 1 hour. Top should be lightly browned.

❖❖❖❖❖❖❖

BRAN MIX CEREAL (Makes 1 quart)

2 cups banana chips
1 cup rye flakes
½ cup slivered almonds
½ cup honey
1 teaspoon vanilla
2 tablespoons vegetable oil
½ cup warm water
¼ teaspoon salt
½ cup blond raisins
1 teaspoon vegetable oil

In large oiled baking dish, place banana chips, rye flakes, and almonds. Combine honey, vanilla, oil, water, and salt in small saucepan, and heat just to boiling point. Pour mixture over dry ingredients, and stir well until everything is moistened. Make layer even in pan. Bake in middle of preheated 300-degree oven for 15 minutes or until fragrance is first noticeable. Then continue to bake mixture, stirring it well every 5 minutes until it is toasted to your taste. Cool in the baking pan. Add raisins, and store in 1 quart glass jar with tight lid.

BARBARA'S MIXED CEREAL (Makes 1 quart)

1 cup rolled oats
½ cup wheat germ
½ cup dried apples cut in small pieces
½ cup dried figs cut in small pieces
½ cup crushed soy nuts
½ cup chopped peanuts
¼ cup sunflower seeds
¼ cup raisins
¼ teaspoon salt

Combine all ingredients, and store in 1 quart glass jar with tight lid. This is the simplest of all cereals because no other preparation is required. Tastes special with ice-cold buttermilk and a sprinkling of maple sugar.

MEUSLI (Serves 1)

4 tablespoons rolled oats
¼ cup light cream
1 apple, washed and grated with the skin on
Juice of 1 lemon
1 tablespoon honey
2 tablespoons finely ground nuts (such as hazelnuts, cashews, almonds)

Soak oats in milk for 5 minutes. Stir in grated apple and lemon juice. Top with honey and nuts. This Swiss classic is one of the quickest fresh breakfasts ever. Vary it by using fruits that are in season.

FRUIT CURRY (Serves 4)

2 pears, sliced
½ honeydew melon, cut in 1-inch pieces
1 banana
½ cantalope, cut in 1-inch pieces
2 navel oranges, cut in sections
10 dates, halved
1 cup white grape juice
1 teaspoon mild curry powder

Combine all ingredients in mixing bowl. Refrigerate at least 2 hours.

VEGETABLE ZIP (Makes 1⅓ cups)

1 fully ripe tomato
½ cup clam juice
2 tablespoons lemon juice
2 shakes Tabasco sauce
½ cup cucumber slices

Place all ingredients in blender, and spin for 10 seconds. Serve over ice.

❖❖❖❖❖❖❖

ROASTED PANCAKES (Serves 4)

1 tablespoon unsalted butter
2 eggs
1 cup milk
1 cup unbleached flour, unsifted
¼ teaspoon salt
¼ cup confectioners' sugar
Fresh seasonal fruit topping (See recipe for Peach Topping.)

Preheat oven to 450 degrees. Place butter in 10-inch quiche pan, and warm for 5 minutes or until it melts. Coat pan completely with melted butter.

In a mixing bowl, beat eggs and milk. Add flour and salt, beating with wire wisk until batter is smooth. Or place eggs, milk, flour, and salt in blender, and spin for 15 seconds on medium speed.

Pour batter into quiche pan, and bake for 15 minutes. Reduce heat to 350 degrees, and bake an additional 7 minutes. The pancake should be puffy and golden brown. Remove from oven and sprinkle with confectioners' sugar. Serve in quiche pan with a selection of fresh fruit toppings.

Peach Topping (Serves 4)

4 cups fresh ripe peaches, sliced
Juice of 1 lemon
½ cup maple sugar
½ teaspoon cinnamon
¼ teaspoon nutmeg
½ stick butter or margarine
½ cup slivered almonds

In medium saucepan, melt butter, and add all ingredients except almonds. Stir over medium heat until peaches are soft and well coated with sugar mixture. Serve over pancakes or ice cream. Top with almonds.

Variations

Variations for sauces include blueberries, raspberries, strawberries or any sweet preserve.

183

❖❖❖❖❖❖❖

LEMON SOUP (Makes 1 quart)

¼ cup cashews, finely chopped
⅛ teaspoon salt
4 tablespoons superfine sugar
3 tablespoons safflower oil
1 small cucumber, peeled and sliced paper-thin
Juice of 4 lemons
1 tablespoon lemon peel, finely grated
3 cups plain yogurt
Water
Lemon slices

Run nuts through a food mill; then combine in a small mixing bowl with salt and sugar. (If you have a mortar and pestle, they are the ideal tools for this procedure.) Add oil 1 tablespoon at a time, until mixture is even-textured. Stir in remaining ingredients except water and lemon slices. Run lemon mixture through blender in batches, each for 30 seconds. Add water to this soup to your preference. Heat through (but do not allow to boil or yogurt will separate) and serve hot, or cover and refrigerate until thoroughly chilled. Garnish with thin lemon slices.

TRIGONA (TRIANGLES)
(Makes approximately 160 2-inch pieces, 40 of each filling)

Cheese Filling

¼ cup Kefalotiri cheese (or Parmesan)
½ pound feta cheese
½ pound cottage cheese
¼ pound cream cheese, at room temperature
3 eggs, well beaten

Grate Kefalotiri, and crumble feta into mixing bowl. Add cottage cheese and cream cheese and combine well. Stir in eggs until mixture is of even texture throughout. Refrigerate 1 hour.

Seafood Filling

¾ pound cooked seafood (such as lobster, crab, shrimp, smoked
    herring)
1½ tablespoons olive oil
1½ tablespoons flour
½ cup milk
¼ cup Gruyère cheese
Dash of cayenne pepper

*Warm olive oil in skillet; then stir in flour. Add milk, cheese, and
cayenne, stirring continuously until mixture is smooth. Remove
from heat, and stir in seafood until well mixed. Cool to room temperature.*

Spinach Filling

1 pound fresh spinach
1 onion, chopped fine and sautéed in olive oil
½ cup grated Swiss cheese
¼ cup pignolia (pine nuts)
3 eggs, well beaten

*Rinse spinach carefully, and discard stems. Shred leaves into
small pieces. Combine spinach, onion, cheese, and pignolia in
mixing bowl. Add eggs, and stir thoroughly.*

Mushroom Filling

½ pound fresh mushrooms
¼ cup onions, diced
6 tablespoons butter
¼ cup fresh parsley, minced
1 teaspoon lemon juice
¼ teaspoon nutmeg
⅛ teaspoon freshly ground black pepper
½ cup sour cream

*Rinse mushrooms, and chop fine. Sauté mushrooms and onion in
4 tablespoons butter over medium heat until onions become
transparent. Stir in parsley, lemon juice, and nutmeg, and stir until
parsley wilts slightly (no more than 1 minute). Remove from heat.
Add pepper, and stir in sour cream.*

To Assemble Trigona

1 pound butter, melted
2 pounds Phyllo pastry

Cut Phyllo into 2- by 5-inch strips, and brush strips individually with melted butter to make them easier to handle and to prevent them from drying out. Place 1 scant teaspoon of filling at end of one strip. Fold the edge over to form a triangle; then turn the triangle over and over to completely encase filling and close all sides of the triangle. Brush both sides with melted butter, and place on cookie sheet sprayed with vegetable cooking spray. Repeat until all filling has been used. Bake in 400-degree oven for 20 minutes or until golden brown. Cool to the touch before serving.

To prepare for freezing, place unbaked triangles in layers in large baking pans, each layer separated from the others with a sheet of aluminum foil. Seal top with a final layer of foil, and place in freezer. When you are ready to bake the trigonas, do not defrost. Bake frozen in preheated 350-degree oven for 25 to 30 minutes. Serve with assorted sauces and dips, such as shrimp paste, lemon sauce or yogurt sauce.

SHRIMP PASTE

1 pound shrimp, cleaned
6 tablespoons butter
2 tablespoons sherry
3 teaspoons lemon juice
3 teaspoons onion, grated
1 teaspoon Dijon mustard
½ teaspoon Tabasco sauce
Capers
2 quarts boiling water

Place raw shrimp in boiling water, and cook for 3 minutes over medium-high heat or until bright pink. Drain on paper towels until completely dry. Chop shrimp very fine; then force pieces through sieve or food mill (a food processor is a blessing at times like this) to make a paste. In large mixing bowl, whip butter until fluffy. Add sherry, lemon juice, onion, mustard, and Tabasco, and mix well. Beat in shrimp paste until mixture is evenly textured. Check seasoning.

Spoon paste into decorative mold or serving dish, and cover with plastic wrap. Refrigerate overnight or at least until paste is firm. To unmold, dip mold in hot water, and run warmed knife around edges to loosen. (If you spray the mold first with vegetable cooking spray, it pops out more easily.) Invert on serving platter, and garnish with capers.

LEMON SAUCE (Makes 1⅓ cups)

¾ cup olive oil
⅓ cup lemon juice
Peel of 2 lemons, grated
1 teaspoon garlic salt
2 bay leaves
⅛ teaspoon white pepper
2 eggs

Place all ingredients in blender, and spin for 10 seconds on medium speed. Refrigerate overnight in glass jar with tight-fitting lid. Shake well before using. Serve at room temperature.

YOGURT SAUCE

1 cup plain yogurt
1 teaspoon garlic salt
2 teaspoons olive oil
1 small cucumber, peeled and grated
½ teaspoon white vinegar

Place all ingredients in blender, and spin for 10 seconds. Serve chilled.

❖❖❖❖❖❖❖

RASPBERRY SHAKE (Serves 4)

1 cup plain yogurt
2 cups raspberries (frozen or fresh)
½ cup sugar
1 teaspoon vanilla
1 tablespoon vegetable oil
⅛ teaspoon salt
1 cup low-fat milk

Place all ingredients in blender, and spin 20 to 30 seconds or until mixture is of uniform texture and color. This is delicious with strawberries, too.

❖❖❖❖❖❖❖

SHREDDED WHEAT BREAD (Makes 2 loaves)

5 shredded wheat biscuits
2 tablespoons butter
¼ cup molasses
2 teaspoons salt
2 cups whole milk, scalded
½ cup warm water
1 package dry yeast
3 cups whole wheat flour
½ cup unbleached flour
Melted butter

Crumble shredded wheat biscuits in large mixing bowl. Add butter, molasses, salt, and milk. Combine well, and allow to cool to room temperature.

Stir in yeast mixture, blending well. Add flours gradually, stirring with spoon or hands until dough leaves sides of bowl. Place dough on floured surface, and knead gently for 3 to 4 minutes. Return dough to bowl, cover it with a damp cloth, and let it rise in a warm spot until it has doubled. Punch dough down, divide it in two, and shape each half into a loaf.

Spray two loaf pans with vegetable cooking spray. Place each loaf into a pan. Cover, and let rise until three-quarters of the way

188

up the sides of the pans. Bake in preheated 375-degree oven for 45 minutes or until golden brown. Remove from oven, and brush with melted butter.

❖❖❖❖❖❖❖

CODDLED EGG (Serves 1)

1 egg
½ strip of bacon, cooked and drained
1 tablespoon shredded mozzarella
1 tablespoon of shredded Cheddar cheese
½ piece of Swiss or Sweet Munchee cheese, torn into small pieces

Spray the inside of the ceramic portion of a coddler with vegetable cooking spray. Drop in bits of bacon. (You can substitute corned beef, pastrami, ham, or salami.) Sprinkle half of the Cheddar and mozzarella, crack in egg, sprinkle with three cheeses, and screw on top of coddler tightly. Place into boiling water up to level of the top of the coddler. Allow to cook for 10 minutes at slow boil. Remove top, and serve. Coddled eggs are wonderful because you make up as many as you need for the day and then wait until your guests appear at the table before you put them in the water to cook.

❖❖❖❖❖❖❖

CONFETTI (Serves 8)

2 cups rice, cooked and chilled
1 cup green seedless grapes, halved
½ cup blond raisins
1 cup pineapple chunks
¾ cup walnuts, broken into small pieces
½ cup maraschino cherries, halved
Juice of 1 lemon
¼ cup mayonnaise
¼ cup plain yogurt
1 avocado sliced thin
1 orange, sliced thin

Combine all ingredients except avocado and orange slices in mixing bowl. Refrigerate at least 2 hours. Transfer to serving dish. Garnish with avocado and orange slices.

CHAPATIS (Indian Flat Bread) (makes 1 dozen)

2 cups whole wheat flour
½ teaspoon salt
2 tablespoons vegetable oil, melted butter, or margarine
½ to ¾ cup cold water
⅓ cup clarified butter (or melted unsalted butter or margarine)

In large mixing bowl, combine flour and salt. Make a well in the dry ingredients, and pour in oil. Mix thoroughly until texture is even. (Your fingers are really the best tools for this because you can feel the little lumps better than with a fork or spoon.) Add ½ cup water, and keep working the dough with your hands until it begins to form a ball. Add additional water, 1 tablespoon at a time, until dough mass is no longer crumbly, but is not sticky.

Turn dough out onto a very lightly floured surface. Knead 8 to 10 minutes or until glossy and elastic. Form dough into 12 even-sized balls, and roll each out into a pancake 7 inches in diameter. (The pancakes will be very thin.)

Brush each Chapati lightly with clarified butter, and cook in a heavy skillet over medium heat for approximately 1 minute. Turn, brush second side, and repeat until Chapati is lightly browned. The Chapati should be flat, so press it down with a spatula if it starts to swell in the pan. Serve hot, or stack and wrap in foil before placing in preheated 200-degree oven for 10 to 15 minutes to hold until you are ready to serve.

POPPY-SEED ROLLS (makes 1 dozen)

1¼ cup warm water
1 package dry yeast or 1 yeast cake
½ teaspoon honey
1 egg, beaten
1¾ cup unbleached flour

¼ cup soy flour
½ cup butter or margarine, softened to room temperature
¼ cup sugar (optional)
1 teaspoon salt
1 cup sautéed onions
½ cup plus 3 tablespoons poppy seeds
Melted butter

Dissolve yeast in warm water and honey. Let mixture sit until bubbles form (called proofing*).*

In large mixing bowl, combine egg, half the flour, ½ cup warm water, ¼ cup butter, sugar, and salt. Beat vigorously for 2 minutes (an electric mixer is a help); then add remaining flour. Mix well. Cover tightly, and refrigerate overnight.

Soak poppy seeds for 1 hour in ½ cup warm water. Remove dough from refrigerator, and punch it down. Roll out on a floured surface into an oblong no more than ½ inch thick. Coat surface with butter, spread onions and drained poppy seeds evenly over the surface, and roll up into a jelly-roll shape (the longer end toward you). With a very sharp, nonserrated knife, cut the roll into 1-inch-thick rounds. Arrange in greased 2-inch muffin cups or a shallow baking pan, with edges of rolls barely touching. Cover rolls with damp towel, and let them rise until doubled in bulk. Brush tops with melted butter, and scatter extra poppy seeds over the tops. Bake in middle of preheated 400-degree oven for 12 to 15 minutes.

❖❖❖❖❖❖❖

RYE CRESCENT ROLLS *(Makes 2 dozen small rolls)*

1 package dry yeast or 1 yeast cake
¼ cup warm water
½ teaspoon honey
1½ cups rye flour
2¾ cups unbleached flour
¼ cup soy flour
¼ cup wheat germ
¾ teaspoon salt
¼ cup sugar or honey
2 eggs, beaten
⅔ cup melted butter
1½ cups sour cream

Dissolve yeast in mixture of warm water and honey. In large mixing bowl, combine all dry ingredients and half the unbleached flour. Make a well in the mixture, and pour in yeast mixture, eggs, ⅓ cup butter, and sour cream. Stir thoroughly; then add remaining flour to form a somewhat sticky dough. Turn dough out onto a floured surface, and knead it until elastic about 8 to 10 minutes. Return dough to bowl, and cover it with damp towel. Let dough rise until doubled, about 1 to 1½ hours. Punch dough down, and divide it into two pieces. Roll out each piece on a floured surface into a thin circle about the size of a small pizza pan. Cut each across the diameter of the circle 6 times, forming 12 triangular wedges. Brush remaining melted butter over wedges. Roll each wedge from the outer edge toward the center of the circle to form a crescent. Bake on foil-lined cookie sheets in middle of preheated 400-degree oven for 20 to 25 minutes or until browned.

❖❖❖❖❖❖❖

POTATO BREAD (Makes two 10-inch round loaves)

2 packages dry yeast or 2 cakes yeast
1 pound potatoes, peeled, boiled, and mashed
3 cups warm water (approximately)
1 teaspoon honey
10 cups unbleached flour
2 teaspoons salt
2 tablespoons olive oil

Dissolve yeast in ½ cup warm water. Proof with honey (let it sit until it bubbles). In large mixing bowl, combine mashed potatoes, flour, salt, and yeast mixture. Add enough warm water to make a smooth, workable dough. Turn dough out onto a very lightly floured surface, and knead it for 10 minutes. Divide dough into two equal pieces. Roll out to fit two 10-inch round baking pans. Oil the pans liberally with olive oil. Transfer dough to pans, and brush light coating of oil on top.

Cover dough with damp cloth, and let it rise 1½ hours or until at least doubled in bulk. Bake in the middle of preheated 400-degree oven for 40 minutes or until golden brown. Cool to room temperature before cutting. This is an old-fashioned Italian peasant bread. Pureed garbanzo beans may be substituted for the potatoes.

❖❖❖❖❖❖❖

WHOLE WHEAT–SUNFLOWER SEED BREAD (Makes 3 loaves)

4½ cups whole milk
¼ cup molasses
¼ cup honey
⅜ cup butter or margarine
2 packages dry yeast or 2 cakes yeast
½ cup warm water
1 cup wheat germ
½ cup sunflower seeds
1 tablespoon salt
12 cups whole wheat flour

In large saucepan, combine milk, molasses, honey, and butter. Warm over medium heat until butter melts, stirring so that molasses and honey blend in. Remove from heat, transfer mixture to very large mixing bowl, and let it cool to lukewarm.

Dissolve yeast in warm water with 1 teaspoon sugar or honey; let it rest until bubbles form. Add to milk mixture. Stir in all other ingredients and 10 cups of the flour. Mix well until dough comes away from the sides of the bowl. Use the remaining 2 cups of flour during the kneading process. Whole wheat requires at least 20 minutes of vigorous kneading in order to develop a fine grain. Butter the mixing bowl, and return dough to it, cover with a damp cloth, and allow it to rise until doubled. Punch dough down. Let it rise again. Punch it down again, and knead it for 5 more minutes. Form dough into 3 loaves.

Butter 3 loaf pans (9 by 5 by 3 inches), and transfer loaves to them. Brush tops with melted butter. Cover with a damp towel, and let dough rise until its nears the top of the pan sides and is rounded on top. Preheat oven to 425 degrees. Place loaves in the middle of the oven, and bake for 15 minutes. Reduce temperature to 350 degrees, and bake another 30 minutes. Bread is done when it recedes from the sides of the pan and sounds hollow when tapped. Turn out of the pan onto rack to cool.

❖❖❖❖❖❖❖

CROUTONS (CHEESE, HERB, AND SWEET)
(Makes about 2 cups each)

1 loaf white bread
1½ cups melted butter or margarine
½ cup finely grated Romano cheese
1 teaspoon parsley flakes
1 teaspoon sage
1 teaspoon garlic powder
½ teaspoon paprika
¼ teaspoon salt
⅛ teaspoon freshly ground black pepper
¼ cup sugar
½ teaspoon cinnamon
½ teaspoon finely grated candied ginger

Cut bread into slices about ½ inch thick. Remove crusts (if desired), and save them for making crumbs. Cut bread into cubes no more than ½ inch on a side. In a large skillet, swirl cubes around in melted butter until all are well coated. Roll a third of cubes in grated cheese. Roll the second third in herb mixture. Roll remaining third in sugar, cinnamon, and ginger. Arrange each variety in a single layer on its own cookie sheet. Bake in middle of preheated 250-degree oven 20 minutes, stirring occasionally to ensure even browning. Store in plastic bags or airtight tins. Use for garnish or in stuffing.

❖❖❖❖❖❖❖

WELSH RAREBIT (Serves 6)

1 tablespoon butter
1 pound sharp Cheddar cheese, grated
1 cup beer
1 teaspoon dry mustard
Water
Pepper to taste
2 egg yolks

In a saucepan or chafing dish, melt butter and cheese. When cheese is partially melted, add beer, and stir until well combined.

Mix mustard with a small amount of water to form a soft paste. Add to cheese mixture along with pepper.

When mixture is slightly thickened, remove from heat, and stir in egg yolks. Serve with hot rolls, bread, or over toast points or English muffins.

❖❖❖❖❖❖❖

RHUBARB FIZZ (Makes 2 quarts)

4 pounds pink rhubarb
6 cups water
1 cup superfine sugar
1 quart ginger ale, chilled
Strawberries or chamomile blossoms
6 sprigs mint

Rinse rhubarb, and cut it into 2-inch pieces, but do not peel it. Place pieces in large pot of water, and bring to a simmer. Cover, and cook over medium heat until very tender, about 30 minutes. Drain liquid into punch bowl, and stir in sugar. Discard pulp.

Chill thoroughly. When ready to serve, add ginger ale. Decorate with strawberries or chamomile blossoms. Pour into frosted, tall glasses over ice cubes, and garnish with mint.

❖❖❖❖❖❖❖

GRAPEFRUIT-AVOCADO CUP (Serves 4)

1 avocado, sliced
1 grapefruit, sectioned
1 cup grapefruit juice

In small serving cups, combine ingredients. Serve chilled.

❖❖❖❖❖❖❖

EGG BURRITOS (Serves 4)

4 eggs, scrambled
4 flour tortillas
1 ripe tomato, sliced
1 ripe avocado, sliced
Salt and pepper to taste

Arrange eggs, tomato, and avocado slices on tortillas. Season to taste. Roll in edges of tortilla to seal. Place on cookie sheet, and warm in 350-degree oven for 5 minutes. Serve hot.

❖❖❖❖❖❖❖

CHEESE STRATA (Serves 6 to 8)

1 large loaf of white bread, crusts removed
8 eggs
2 cups milk
½ stick butter, melted
½ teaspoon dry mustard
6 ounces crumbled Cheddar cheese
6 ounces crumbled mozzarella cheese
4 large slices Swiss cheese, torn into small pieces
Vegetable cooking spray

Spray a 9-by-12-inch roasting pan with vegetable cooking spray. Line pan with one layer of white bread. Sprinkle half of the three cheeses over the bread. Add a second layer of bread and the remainder of the cheese. In a medium-size bowl, mix the eggs, melted butter, milk, and dry mustard well. Pour mixture over the bread and cheese. Cover pan with plastic wrap, and refrigerate overnight.

In the morning, remove plastic wrap, and bake in preheated 350-degree oven for 45 minutes to 1 hour. Top should be lightly brown.

This is a wonderful recipe for a large group who all want breakfast at the same time. It needs to be served immediately, once it starts to cool, it will fall and lose its visual appeal.

❖❖❖❖❖❖❖

OMELETS BY THE DOZEN

You may vary your omelets by incorporating cheeses, vegetables, potatoes, grains, or pasta; by making them folded (French), puffed (Spanish), or served in wedges (Italian); and by serving them with sauces. The combinations could keep you experimenting in the kitchen for weeks. Here are a dozen variations to begin with.

Basic French Omelet (Serves 2)

4 eggs (Use no more in a single omelet, or it will be difficult to
   handle.)
¼ cup water
2 tablespoons butter
Salt
Pepper

Beat eggs gently in medium-size bowl. Add water, and stir until mixture is of even consistency. Melt butter over low to medium heat in 8-inch skillet, tilting pan so butter coats sides about halfway up. Pour in egg mixture. When eggs begin to set, lift up edges all around with a spatula and tilt pan so uncooked mixture runs beneath the cooked. Eggs should not stick to the bottom of the pan. If this starts to happen, reduce heat, and slide a bit more butter into the pan when you lift eggs from the bottom. High heat makes eggs toughen, so treat the omelet very gently.

When the bottom of the omelet is a golden brown and the top is almost set but not runny, slide spatula under one half, and flip it over on top of the other half. Ease the folded omelet onto a heated plate, season to taste, and serve at once.

197

Omelet with Herbs (Serves 2)

Choose one of the following combinations:

1 teaspoon fresh parsley and 1 teaspoon fresh chives
1 teaspoon dill and 1 teaspoon prepared mustard
¼ teaspoon garlic powder and ½ teaspoon oregano
¼ teaspoon sage and ¼ teaspoon thyme
¼ teaspoon rosemary and ¼ teaspoon nutmeg

Mince fresh herbs, or crush dried. Add one combination to Basic French Omelet just before folding. Serve at once.

Omelet with Cheese (Serves 2)

4 ounces of your favorite cheese

Grate cheese, and add to Basic French Omelet about 1 minute before you fold it. Cheese should be melted but not running out of the edges of the omelet. Serve at once.

Omelet with Onions (Serves 2)

1 Bermuda onion
2 tablespoons butter

Slice onion very thin, and sauté in butter in separate skillet over medium heat. Do not use high heat, or butter and onion will scorch. When onion slices are transparent, remove skillet from heat, and set aside while you prepare eggs. Add onions to omelet about 1 minute before folding. Serve at once.

Omelet with Mushrooms (Serves 2)

4 ounces fresh mushrooms
3 tablespoons butter
1 tablespoon fresh parsley, chopped
½ cup yogurt

Slice mushrooms very thin, and sauté in butter in a separate skillet over medium heat for 5 minutes. Remove from heat, and fold in parsley and yogurt. Return skillet to heat until yogurt is warmed through, but do not allow mixture to bubble because excessive heat destroys many nutritional factors in the yogurt. Add mushroom mixture to Basic French Omelet as eggs begin to set. Fold, and serve at once.

Omelet with Fried Peppers (Serves 2)

2 cups sweet or hot peppers
¼ cup olive oil
¼ teaspoon garlic powder

Slice peppers into thin rounds, and sauté in olive oil in separate covered skillet over low to medium heat until peppers are soft. Stir occasionally to prevent scorching. Sprinkle garlic powder on peppers. Add peppers to Basic French Omelet just before folding. Serve at once.

Omelet with Green Beans (Serves 2)

1 cup green beans
Juice of 1 lemon
¼ cup slivered almonds

Steam green beans until they are fork-tender. Squeeze lemon juice over the beans. Fold in almonds. Add mixture to Basic French Omelet as eggs begin to set. Fold, and serve at once.

Omelet with Marinated Artichokes (Serves 2)

4 marinated artichokes (Spanish, in jars)

Add artichokes to Basic French Omelet just before folding. Serve at once.

Omelet with Spinach and Feta Cheese (Serves 2)

½ cup fresh spinach, cleaned
¼ cup feta cheese, crumbled
¼ cup toasted bread crumbs
¼ teaspoon nutmeg

Steam spinach until just softened. In mixing bowl, combine spinach, cheese, bread crumbs, and nutmeg. Add to Basic French Omelet as eggs begin to set. Fold, and serve at once.

Omelet with Potatoes (Serves 2)

1 large baked potato
1 tablespoon minced fresh parsley
2 tablespoons olive oil
¼ teaspoon vinegar
2 tablespoons Bakon (tastes like bacon but is made from nutritional yeast)

Cut potato into ½-inch cubes, leaving skin on. In mixing bowl, combine potato and all other ingredients. Let rest for 15 minutes before putting in omelet. Add to Basic French Omelet just before folding. Serve at once.

Omelet with Olives and Pimento (Serves 2)

¼ cup black or green olives (Greek, Spanish, or Italian)
2 pimento pods (in jar)
2 tablespoons freshly grated Romano or Parmesan cheese

Cut olives into slivers, descarding pits. Slice pimentos into thin strips. In mixing bowl, combine olives, pimentos, and cheese. Add to Basic French Omelet as eggs begin to set. Fold, and serve at once.

❖❖❖❖❖❖❖

APPLE TART (Serves 6)

Crust

2 ½ cups unbleached flour, sifted
1 tablespoon baking powder
1 teaspoon salt
1 cup butter, chilled
¼ cup lard, chilled
½ to ¾ cup ice water

Place flour and salt and baking powder in large mixing bowl. Cut in butter and lard with fork or pastry cutter. (Do not use your fingers because that warms dough.) Add half the ice water as necessary to make dough come cleanly away from the sides of the bowl. Roll out on a lightly floured surface to be just slightly larger than a 12-inch tart pan.

Filling

6 medium McIntosh or other tart apples, peeled and sliced
2 eggs
1 ¼ cups sugar
½ cup whipping cream
½ cup whole milk
⅛ teaspoon salt
2 egg whites
1 cup slivered almonds

Arrange apple slices in circular pattern, their sides just touching, to cover the bottom of crust. Bake in preheated 350-degree oven for 20 minutes.

In mixing bowl, combine 2 eggs, ¼ cup sugar, cream, and milk. Pour over apples after baking 20 minutes. Return tart to oven for another 20 minutes until top is golden brown and knife inserted comes out clean. Cool to warm.

In small saucepan, mix egg whites, almonds, and 1 cup sugar over medium heat. Stir continuously until mixture starts to congeal. Pour over cooled tart, and spread evenly over top.

201

HOMEMADE SAUSAGE (Makes 6 pounds)

6 pounds lean pork
6 teaspoons salt
3 teaspoons freshly ground black pepper
4 teaspoons sage
½ teaspoon thyme
1 teaspoon paprika

Run all ingredients through a meat grinder twice. Shape into patties, and freeze until needed. Bake on a cookie sheet at 450 degrees for 20 to 25 minutes or until cooked completely through. By making your own sausage meat, you will avoid the preservatives so widely used in commercial sausages.

GREEN TOMATO PIE (2 pies, each serves 4 to 6)

4 piecrusts (Frozen will do nicely, once thawed.)
8 to 10 very hard green tomatoes
2 very large onions, sliced and sautéed in ½ stick sweet butter
Italian seasoned bread crumbs
Coarse salt
Freshly ground pepper
2 tablespoons brown sugar (approximately)
1 pound Swiss cheese
1 pound Muenster cheese
Wine vinegar

Prepare two crusts. Into each, sprinkle bread crumbs. Layer tomato slices, cheese, and sautéed onions. Sprinkle each layer with coarse salt, pepper, and brown sugar. Repeat until pie shells are full. (Depending on size of tomatoes and onions, this may even fill a third pie shell.) Top with more bread crumbs and a sprinkle of wine vinegar. Put top crust on each pie. Crimp edges and slash. Bake at 375 degrees until brown. Brushing top with milk as pie starts to brown will glaze it nicely. This pie freezes very well. It can be made all summer into early fall when green tomatoes are in your garden, frozen, and served all winter as a very hearty main dish for a skier's or hunter's breakfast.

10

Interviews with Successful Hosts

When I say that a host is successful, I don't mean that he or she makes a lot of money from Bed and Breakfast. Some do, of course, but what makes for success in this business is satisfaction. Successful hosts are people for whom the B&B life-style is enriching and satisfying. Guests find them welcoming and hospitable. Reservation services get rave reviews for feedback and find working with these hosts a pleasure because they are cooperative, respond promptly, and always follow through on their commitments.

The stories in this chapter are based on conversations I had with successful hosts, who told me why they went into B&B and shared some interesting anecdotes with me. They also shared tips for new hosts. I hope that these glimpses into others' lives will illustrate the variety of people involved in the B&B movement and perhaps touch on your situation, as well.

BARBARA OF SAN FRANCISCO, CALIFORNIA

When I was in San Francisco in 1986 at a trade association meeting, I attended a cocktail party given by a hostess of American Family Inn Bed & Breakfast, our San Francisco affiliate. The cocktail party was an inspired marketing tool for Barbara's B&B because it gave the heads of forty reservation services from across the United States and Canada a chance to tour her home. I now know it from firsthand experience, and I have vividly described it to many of my clients and specifically asked for this home when booking guests in San Francisco.

Barbara's story of becoming a hostess is an example at the luxury end of the spectrum. Her husband has run a successful business for many years. They owned a lovely home that was decorated with the help of a professional. One day, her decorator phoned to say, "Barbara, darling! You know that on a scale of one to ten, your house is a four. The house across the street from me needs total redecoration, but even before that it's an eight! It's for sale, and you must buy it." Well, the house was sold to Barbara on the courthouse steps for $563,000. The owner had previously turned down $800,000 in hopes of getting $1 million. Barbara and her decorator then went off to Europe, where they spent $250,000 acquiring fabulous period furniture and even custom-made silk wallpaper. The house is a showplace. The area is escalating in price every day. If she decides to sell, her equity will have skyrocketed. Meantime, she enjoys offering gracious hospitality to her guests at rates ranging from $75 to $125 a night. On weekends, they enjoy the culinary delights of a French chef.

SY AND DONNA OF TEMPE, ARIZONA

Sy and Donna have a ranch-style home and use two of their four bedrooms for B&B. Donna is at home. Sy is a semiretired professor of law who teaches part-time. Donna makes superb bagels. In February 1985, with their children grown, they were thinking about traveling by doing some home exchanges. Then they read an article in an Arizona magazine about Bed and Breakfast and thought, "Let's look into this." They interviewed

the two reservation services covering Tempe and chose to affiliate with Ruth Young's Mi Casa Su Casa Bed & Breakfast Reservation Service.

Once they decided to open their home, their close friends
were supportive and thought they would make perfect hosts.
Friends not so close to them reacted very differently. They said,
"You mean you'll be letting strangers into your home?" Donna
says they thought she and Sy were "bananas."

Hosting has worked out very well for them. They average
about ten guests a month. The usual stay is about three days.
Donna estimates that they earn about $2,500 a year from the
business, which they see as a wonderful hobby that has introduced them to people from all over the world. She and Sy have
taken guests to the symphony and welcomed them at holiday
parties. And needless to say, *they* are welcome guests the world
over. They still correspond with many of the people they have
met. One man, a professor from Philadelphia, Pennsylvania,
they found exceptionally interesting. He was part French and
part Sioux Indian. The classic absentminded professor, he got
lost in the airport, and it took them over an hour to find him.
After ten days of basking in the sun, he went back home really
looking like a full-blooded Sioux and chuckling about the ex-
pressions on his colleagues' faces. Sy and Donna get letters
from him from all over the world. Most of the time starting out,
"As usual I'm lost."

Donna's tips to new hosts: "Like people. Have empathy for
different kinds of people. Some people want to be left alone;
others really respond to being included as part of the family."
She could not report one bad experience.

JONI OF ANNAPOLIS, MARYLAND

Joni is single. She is a self-employed kitchen designer who
makes her home in the historic district of Annapolis. She has
been a host for one year and works with Travellers Reservation

Service. She has one room available for guests but sometimes makes her master bedroom available, too. This is a seasonal area. In season (April through October), she has guests about three days a week; off-season, only four days a month. She estimates that she earns about $3,000 a year from B&B.

Why did Joni open her home? "For the fun of it. To meet people. They all seem to have interesting backgrounds and life-styles. I get a lot of people involved in boating and sailing because I live so close to the bay, and the naval academy. Many of these people have offered to open their homes to me and have become friends.

Her tip for new hosts: Be sure to let the people know that your home is their home and that they can come and go and share with you.

NORMA OF COLORADO SPRINGS, COLORADO

Norma and her husband have a two-level home in the foothills at the edge of Colorado Springs. One side of the home overlooks the town; the other side offers fabulous mountain views. The full lower level is available for guests, as is one room with bath on the upper level. The lower level has two bedrooms, a bath, a recreation room, and a hot tub. Both levels have forty-foot decks. Once their youngest daughter went off to college, this couple found that having all these bedrooms got lonely. Norma wanted to keep the house for holiday times, when her brood and their offspring come home and fill it up with joy. But because the extra space was often empty, she felt B&B would give her something to do and would be a social outlet as well.

To prepare for guests, Norma was lucky. All she needed to do was get some new linens and some extra-thick cotton bathrobes for use near the hot tub. In the summer, she has guests 50 percent of the time; in winter, only 15 to 20 percent.

Her friends thought she was crazy to welcome strangers,

but Norma says that all her guests have been screened by her reservation service, B&B Rocky Mountains, and that she has never had a problem guest. The $4,800 a year she earns pay her daughter's college expenses, and Norma has made great friends. She says, "Hosting is like being on vacation without having to go on vacation. You get the stimulation of meeting many people from different cultures and backgrounds."

SUSAN AND TOM OF WEST SHOKAN, NEW YORK

Although she grew up in rural Ulster County, New York, in the Catskill Mountains about two and a half hours north of New York City, Susan never expected to be a farmer's wife. Tom, who teaches in the local high school, is a farmer at heart. A few years ago, they moved back to Ulster County from the city and bought a farm. Farm life is not easy. They raise some sheep, pigs, beef cattle, and ducks and board a few horses. Taking care of the animals means being home every day. Two years ago, they opened two rooms of their home to guests. They are members of Bed & Breakfast U.S.A. They are open all year, do most of their business on weekends, and earn about $8,000 a year from guests who enjoy farm hospitality. One guest room has a double bed and a fireplace and is very appealing for a romantic getaway. The other room has a king-size bed and two single beds, which makes it perfect for families who want to show their children country life. Guests are encouraged to meet the animals, explore the land, and hike or go antiquing nearby. And they are treated to gigantic country breakfasts that include the sausages, bacon, and jams that Susan and Tom make themselves.

Susan finds hosting very rewarding. A Japanese couple stays with them each season. "We prepare dinner for them one night, and they bring all the fixings and cook us an oriental feast on the other" Susan says, beaming. One of Susan's favorite guests was a soap opera star who stayed with them many weekends till she bought a house nearby. Now she's a neighbor and boards her horse with Susan. Susan still gets to know the soap's plot before everyone else and relishes her secret.

Asked about problems, Susan reports only one difficult party of guests, a couple with two very unruly children. When she accepted the booking and spoke to the guests, she made it very clear that with fireplaces, wood-burning stoves, and animals around, children must be careful and well controlled. She also needed to be assured that the children would not disturb other guests. Although the parents had said there would be no problem, the children were totally out of control. Susan finally had to take them aside and tell them that if they didn't follow house rules, she would have to ask their parents to take them and leave. Once she did this, there were no further problems.

Susan's tips for new hosts: Contact a good reservation service. Talk to other hosts in your area.

BOB AND BETTY OF ROCKY MOUNTAINS SKI AREA

Bob and Betty have been running their B&B for three years through Bed & Breakfast Rocky Mountains. They have a two-story, five-bedroom, four-bath home in the mountains convenient to skiing. Their home is unique in that the three guest bedrooms (which share two baths) have separate entrances and are each on separate levels, giving both hosts and guests lots of privacy. Bob and Betty, who are retired, became hosts after talking to friends at church who were hosts. To ready their house, they had little more to do than put privacy locks on the bedroom doors. Bob works with the local chamber of commerce but takes guests only from the reservation service. He feels that the chamber does no screening and doesn't understand the personal nature of the host/guest relationship.

Bob tells an amusing story about a guest, Helen, who arrived a few minutes before he and Betty had to leave the house to take a friend to the Denver airport, a two-hour ride away. They greeted Helen, showed her to her accommodations, apologized for having to run out right away, and said they would get acquainted when they returned in the evening. They dropped their friend at the airport and headed home only to find that the road back was blocked by a large snowslide. They had to go back to Denver and spend the night with friends. They felt a little trepidation about the fact that a total stranger was alone at their home. They called Helen and told her what had happened. Her reply was, "Would it be okay if I lock the doors here?" They relaxed. Helen took good care of their home and welcomed them with gracious hospitality on their return the next day.

Bob's only problem, one he's afraid is unsolvable, is that although he and Betty have a 4:00 to 6:00 P.M. arrival time, many of their guests fly in for the skiing, because of bad weather (the kind that's good for skiing), the planes are late, and guests sometimes arrive very late.

Their tips for new hosts: If you like to meet and greet, hosting is for you. Use the best agency you can find.

ARTHUR OF NEW YORK CITY

Arthur's Co-op studio apartment near Lincoln Center can sleep up to four people. He read about a course I teach in New York City, decided to take it, and began hosting a year ago. He has guests about twice a month for three or four days at a time. During these times, he stays at his girlfriend's apartment nearby. Arthur always tries to greet his guests personally and orient them to the apartment, the neighborhood, and New York City before leaving them to the privacy of their home away from home in the big city. He has prepared an album for guests. Each page, covered with plastic to keep it fresh, describes an aspect of city life, such as nearby restaurants, emergency numbers, theater, and nightlife. This helps a lot but is most useful as a follow-up to a warm welcome and personally showing guests around the apartment.

In his first year as a host, Arthur earned about $5,000 plus the tax benefits of using his home for business while building equity in it. He has enjoyed meeting a diverse group of people and has had no problem guests. He has even had children stay. Once he returned to find a note from a parent apologizing because her two-year-old rearranged Arthur's bookshelves. "No harm done," he chuckles.

Arthur says an extra benefit of B&B is learning how to clean his apartment and take pride in it. One day, his housekeeper was ill and couldn't come. When she called, he was already dressed and ready to walk out the door to work. Instead, still dressed, he scrubbed out the bathtub. He caught sight of himself in suit and tie bent over the tub and laughed as he realized that he was enjoying it.

Arthur's tips for those who want to offer their places unhosted: Make yourself available, if you can, to meet and greet your guests. Let them know where you can be reached for questions or in an emergency. If you can't do all this, get someone else to stand in for you.

ARLENE AND NORMAN OF SACO, MAINE

Arlene and Norman have lived on a dairy farm most of their adult life. Their beautiful old farmhouse sits atop hundreds of acres, including a stretch of the Saco River and an old Indian burial ground. Their children are grown, but one son still lives at home. In 1986, the farm could no longer support itself. Norman sold most of his stock and turned the fields to raising feed for others' animals. Arlene heard about B&B and thought it might be a good way to supplement their income during this transitional period.

They opened on July 4, 1986. During the summer, they had thirty-two guests, which earned them about $800. They use two rooms and a bath for guests and serve a sensational country breakfast. Around Labor Day, business dropped off. Fearing that B&B was just a summer business, Arlene took a job. But as fall progressed, weekend guests started coming, and Arlene and Norman earned another $400 before the year was out.

Norman went along with Arlene at the start, mostly to keep peace, and figured that this interest in B&B would pass, that it was something to do until the farm became self-sufficient again. But now it is the number-one thing they both enjoy doing. They have plans to purchase two beautiful Clydesdale horses to pull their sled in winter and their wagon in summer, something that guests can enjoy as part of their farm experience. When we visited them with our six-year-old daughter, a new calf had just been born, and we were invited to help milk the cows and meet the newest calf and all the other animals.

Arlene and Norman are part of B&B Maine Reservation Service, but many guests come from local referrals because they are well known in the community. An article about them in a local paper was picked up by some other papers in neighboring states and has resulted in many bookings. So far, there have been no bad guests or problems. Arlene reports having both children and pets visit. They have even rescued their old crib from the attic, along with some other baby gear. And they are looking forward to continued growth as their business matures.

MILDRED OF SEATTLE, WASHINGTON

Mildred has managed a B&B in her 1890 Victorian home for six years. She has three rooms and one and a half baths available for guests on the second floor and a small apartment on the ground floor. She and her husband had looked into the prospect of opening their home but decided against it because her husband was reluctant to give keys to strangers and didn't want to wait up at night for guests to come home.

When her husband became ill, a big, burly male nurse joined their household. Mildred felt that he could wait up for guests, so she joined Irmgard Castleberry's Pacific Bed & Breakfast Agency. The first four guests were so wonderful that Mildred soon forgot her qualms about having strangers in their home. After her husband's death, she decided that being a B&B host would help her adjust to widowhood. It did indeed give her a new outlook on life. Her friends were supportive, but her brother-in-law said, "One of these days, you're going to get it." After many years of consistently wonderful guests, her brother-in-law stopped being the voice of doom. Mildred's business now helps her maintain her historic home and introduces her to new friends from all over. Mildred encourages her guests to share breakfast together for they find many interesting things in common. One morning, she had a young lady from Jerusalem at the table with some people from Munster, Indiana and they found out that they had a mutual friend.

Mildred feels that B&B people are different, nicer than most. "Wild party types," she says, "prefer hotels." One woman who came for a one-week stay arrived on a Sunday. Mildred had corresponded with her to make the arrangements for her visit and knew that she was forty-seven years old, had had a stroke, had some difficulty with speech, and was partially paralyzed. Mildred understood that this woman needed someone around to talk to and arranged for Bonnie, her house-sitter, to greet the guest on arrival and spend the following weekend at the house while Mildred was away attending a family celebration. Bonnie even took the guest to the airport. A few weeks later, Bonnie received a letter from the woman she had befriended. The letter informed her that this woman had a considerable inheritance which she neither needed nor wanted and which she had decided to share with people who had been kind to her. For years now, Bonnie has been receiving $50 a month from this grateful guest.

Another family came for their son's wedding. Mildred was very helpful to them and their friends and even invited two sons who were not staying with her to join their parents for breakfast. When they left, Mildred found a $100 tip with a note of thanks for her warmth, hospitality, and good advice.

She too, reports no bad experiences. She did, however, have one guest who came for a night but stayed nineteen days. Mildred had difficulty convincing this young woman to leave; she felt too at home to move on.

Mildred's guests come to her from two reservation services and the Washington Department of Tourism. She has lots of repeat business and many referrals from satisfied guests. She treats guests very specially. One half hour before breakfast, she knocks on bedroom doors and leaves orange juice and coffee.

Her tip to new hosts: Be relaxed and warm.

ELSIE OF HANOVER, NEW JERSEY

Elsie and her husband live in a large 200-year-old colonial house with a pool and beautifully landscaped grounds in Hanover, near Morristown. When their children grew up, they considered selling the rambling house and buying a condominium, but they didn't really want to move. The house was ready for redecorating and when Elsie looked into B&B, she saw a business that would keep her right where she wanted to be. The tax breaks would enable her to redecorate. She gave extra attention to the two guest rooms, one very feminine, the other very masculine. Both have private baths.

They opened in November 1985 and have guests about twice a month. So far, they've had four sets of honeymooners who have enjoyed the pool and the privacy of the estate. One set of guests came on their way back from a celebrity wedding. Elsie knew where they had been and was dying to ask about the wedding but didn't want to seem pushy. Finally, the guests asked, "Don't you want to hear about the wedding?" They all laughed and exchanged lots of gossip.

Elsie earned about $3,000 in her first year of business. She likes to have short-term guests, people who stay no longer than two weeks. She got the idea of opening her home from her own stays at B&B's in New England. She doesn't work outside the home, so for her the business is an opportunity to meet people. Her husband enjoys it, too, but it's really Elsie's thing.

Their friends didn't understand what B&B was in the beginning and couldn't understand Elsie "taking in boarders." Elsie laughs at the term; she considers guests who pay $66 to $76 a night very elegant boarders, indeed. She is very selective and takes guests only through her reservation service, Bed & Breakfast of New Jersey.

PEGGY OF LAFAYETTE, LOUISIANA

Peggy and her husband have an 1880 Cajun Victorian home at the edge of plantation country. The house was built by a wealthy French farmer in Acadian French style. Guests enjoy two bedrooms and bath, the parlor, and a glass-enclosed porch. Peggy is a teacher; her husband, a petroleum engineer. They opened their B&B a year ago after returning from a trip to the wine country of California and experiencing B&B's there. Before the trip, Peggy thought that without thirty rooms, there wasn't any point to opening your home; but in California she saw that private homes with only a few guest rooms offered a more intimate charm. Her husband was skeptical. He said, "Go ahead, but you must realize nobody's going to come." Friends were sure Peggy would be raped and murdered. So far, they have had no bad experiences.

Once Peggy's husband saw that guests were indeed discovering their place, his next fear was that Peggy would get $50 for her room and then take the guests out for $100 dinners, generous soul that she is. He told her, "The first time you invite the guests to our club and put dinner on my account, we close our doors." Naturally, Peggy had a big smile on her face when she heard her husband inviting guests from Nantucket to the club for dinner. Asked how her friends feel about her B&B now, Peggy replies, "They're jealous as all get out."

Peggy has earned about $7,200 from her B&B efforts this year. She is busiest in spring and fall, when the flowers are in bloom. She does lots of local business connected with weddings and other celebrations. Her tourist trade comes mainly from New England, the Washington, D.C., area, and California. She finds B&B guests have big hearts and souls. Some people arrive carrying fresh apricots from California or fresh-baked bread. "Under Louisiana law, we are considered a boardinghouse, but our guests are hardly the type that would frequent a boarding-house."

Peggy's guests have been extremely interesting. One gentleman was an engineer from NASA. He sat in front of the blazing fire one evening and told Peggy and her husband his nightmare, in graphic detail, of what could happen during a launch. "This was months before the Challenger disaster. As we were watching on TV, we saw his worst nightmare happening."

"Most guests share happier stories with us," says Peggy. "This Christmas I'm giving watches that are selling in the stores for $100. One of my guests put me in touch with a Hong Kong wholesaler who got them for me at $22." Asked if she ever has problem guests, Peggy replied, "Our only problem is some reservation requests from local residents thinking they will use our place for an affair. Since we know so many people in the community, we don't want to be privy to this type of secret. We have to subtly convey that they probably won't be happy at our place."

Her tips: Hosting requires trust. Don't open your home if you have a suspicious nature.

CAROL AND TIMOTHY OF MONTCLAIR, NEW JERSEY

Carol is a divorced schoolteacher, with an eight-year-old son. Carol also tutors and attends school herself but welcomes her B&B guests both to supplement the family income and to meet people. She describes the experience as a very positive one that has helped her to teach responsibility to her son, Timothy. He helps set the table and put the rolls in a basket because most mornings Carol leaves before the guests come down for breakfast. They find the coffee plugged in, the table set, and breakfast waiting.

Carol has one room for guests. She charges $40 for a single, $45 for a double, and a special monthly rate of $600 for corporate guests. In her first year, she estimates that she will earn $2,500. Three of her guests this year have been long-term corporate guests who were there during the week but went home on weekends. Tourists have visited from many parts of the world. A few have brought children. Short-term visitors with children have worked out well with her son. One child was Israeli and spoke very little English. It was amusing to watch him play with Timothy and his friends. Once, they were playing the card game War with a youngster who was cheating. Timothy kept telling this boy not cheat, and suddenly the Israeli boy said in perfect English, "Robby, stop cheating!"

Carol's first guest was a world traveler who, upon hearing that she was planning at trip to the West Coast, prepared a detailed itinerary for her that included places to stay, restaurants, routes to travel, and people to call. Later, he sent her travel brochures. She took the trip and followed many of his recommendations; they were wonderful.

Not all of Carol's friends liked the idea of her opening her home to guests. Others said they, too, were interested. All were curious to see who would come. Carol didn't ask their advice but presented her decision as a fait accompli. She discovered B&B of New Jersey while reading a B&B book to plan a trip to Nantucket. Her guests come to her from her reservation service and through word of mouth.

Her tip for hosts with children: "Be careful about long-term guests bringing children. Although such situations are uncommon, the mix with your children can become a problem after the novelty wears off."

YOU OF YOURTOWN, U.S.A.

Once you've used this book to open your home to B&B guests, I'd like to hear your story. Who knows, the next edition may include your tips and anecdotes. Write to Barbara Notarius, Bed & Breakfast, U.S.A., Ltd., P.O. Box 606, Croton-on-Hudson, NY 10520.

Appendix

Bed & Breakfast
Reservation Services Worldwide

UNITED STATES

ALABAMA

Bed & Breakfast Montgomery
P.O. Box 886
Milbrook, Al 36054
(205) 285-5421

ALASKA

Alaska Private Lodgings
(Anchorage and surrounding areas)
1236 West 10th Avenue
Anchorage, AK 99501
(907) 258-1717

Stay with a Friend Bed & Breakfast Service
(Alaska and Hawaii)
3605 Artic Boulevard 173
Anchorage, AK 99503
(907) 344-4006

ARKANSAS

Bed & Breakfast of Arkansas Ozarks White River Landing, Inc.
White River Landing Inc.
Route 1, Box 38
Calico Rock, AR 72519
(501) 297-8764

ARIZONA

Mi Casa Su Casa
(Arizona, Utah, California)
P.O. Box 950
Tempe, AZ 85281
(602) 990-0682

CALIFORNIA

American Family Inn Bed & Breakfast San Francisco
(Greater San Francisco and wine and gold country)
P.O. Box 349
San Francisco, CA 94101
(415) 931-3083

America's CoHost Bed & Breakfast
P.O. Box 9302
Whittier, CA 90608
(213) 699-8427

Bed & Breakfast International
(San Francisco and West Coast)
151 Ardmore Road
Kensington, CA 94707
(415) 525-4569

Bed & Breakfast of Los Angeles
(Los Angeles and California coastline)
32074 Waterside Lane
Westlake Village, CA 91361
(818) 889-7325 or 889-8870

Bed & Breakfast of Southern California
1943 Sunny Crest Drive 304
Fullerton, CA 92635
(714) 738-8361

California Houseguests, Intl. Inc.
(Statewide)
18653 Ventura Boulevard 190
Tarzana, CA 91356
(818) 344-7878

Eye Openers Bed & Breakfast Reservations
(Statewide)
P.O. Box 694
Altadena, CA 91001
(213) 684-4428 or (818) 797-2055

COLORADO

Bed & Breakfast Rocky Mountains
(Colorado, New Mexico, Utah, Montana, Wyoming)
P.O. Box 804
Colorado Springs, CO 80901
(303) 630-3433

Bed & Breakfast Vail Valley
(Ski areas)
P.O. Box 491
Vail, CO 81658
(303) 949-1212

CONNECTICUT

Nutmeg Bed & Breakfast
(Statewide and specializing in executive relocation)
222 Girard Avenue
Hartford, CT 06105
(203) 236-6698

DELAWARE

Bed & Breakfast of Delaware
Box 177, 3650 Silverside Road
Wilmington, DE 19810
(302) 479-9500

DISTRICT OF COLUMBIA

The Bed & Breakfast League
(District of Columbia and suburbs)
3639 Van Ness Street NW
Washington, DC 20008
(202) 363-7767

FLORIDA

Tropical Isles Bed & Breakfast
Box 382
Key Biscayne, FL 33149
(305) 361-3956

GEORGIA

Bed & Breakfast Atlanta
1801 Piedmont Avenue #208
Atlanta, GA 30324
(404) 875-0525 or 875-9672

ILLINOIS

Bed & Breakfast/Chicago, Inc.
P.O. Box 14088
Chicago, IL 60614
(312) 951-0085

Prairie Hospitality, Inc.
(Statewide)
P.O. Box 3035
Oak Park, IL 60303
(312) 386-8620

IOWA

Bed & Breakfast in Iowa
(Statewide)
Box 430
Preston, IA 52069
(319) 689-4222

KANSAS

Kansas City Bed & Breakfast
(Kansas and Missouri)
P.O. Box 14781
Lenexa, KS 66215
(913) 268-4214

KENTUCKY

Kentucky Homes Bed & Breakfast
(Statewide)
1431 St. James Court
Louisville, KY 40208
(502) 635-7341

Ohio Valley Bed & Breakfast
(Ohio, Kentucky, Indiana)
6876 Taylor Mill Road
Independence, KY 41051
(606) 356-7865

LOUISIANA

Bed & Breakfast, Inc.
(New Orleans)
1360 Moss Street Box 52257
New Orleans, LA 70152-2257
(504) 525-4640

Southern Comfort Bed & Breakfast Reservation Service
(Louisiana, Mississippi, Florida, New Mexico, and Acapulco, Mexico)
2856 Hundred Oaks
Baton Rouge, LA 70808
(504) 346-1928 or (504) 928-9815

MAINE

Bed & Breakfast Down East, Ltd.
(Statewide and Canadian Maritime Provinces)
Box 547, Macomber Mill Road
Eastbrook, ME 04634
(207) 565-3517

Bed & Breakfast of Maine
(Statewide)
32 Colonial Village
Falmouth, ME 04105
(207) 781-4528 (nights and weekends, answering machine at
other times)

MASSACHUSETTS

B&B Associates Bay Colony Ltd.
(Statewide)
P.O. Box 166 Babson Park Branch
Boston, MA 02157
(617) 449-5302

B&B Boston (Professional conferences and
seminars at Harvard and MIT only)
16 Ballard Street
Newton Center, MA 02159
(617) 332-4199

Bed & Breakfast Marblehead & Northshore
54 Amherst Road
Beverly, MA 01915
(617) 921-1336

Berkshire Bed & Breakfast Homes
106 South Street
Williamsburg, MA 01091

Greater Boston Hospitality
Box 1142
Brookline, MA 02140
(617) 277-5430

House Guests of Cape Cod
(Cape Cod, Nantucket, and Martha's Vineyard)
P.O. Box AR
Dennis, MA 02638
(617) 896-7053

MICHIGAN

Betsy Ross Bed & Breakfast in Michigan
(Statewide)
P.O. Box 1731
Dearborn, MI 48121
(313) 561-6041

MINNESOTA

Special Places
(Minnesota and Wisconsin)
4624 Highland Road
Minnetonka, MN 55345
(612) 938-3326

MISSISSIPPI

Lincoln Ltd. Bed & Breakfast
(Statewide)
P.O. Box 3479
Meridan, MS 39303
(601) 482-5483

NEBRASKA

Bed & Breakfast of Nebraska
(Statewide)
1464 28th Avenue
Columbus, NE 68601
(402) 564-7591

NEW HAMPSHIRE

New Hampshire Bed & Breakfast
(Statewide)
R.F.D. 3, Box 53
Laconia, NH 03246
(603) 279-8348

NEW JERSEY

Bed & Breakfast of New Jersey
(Statewide)
Suite 132, 103 Godwin Avenue
Midland Park, NJ 07432
(201) 444-7409

NEW MEXICO

BBB Bed & Breakfast
436 Sunset
Santa Fe, NM 87501
(505) 983-3523

NEW YORK

Bed & Breakfast Leatherstocking Reservations
(Central New York)
389 Brockway Road
Frankfort, NY 13340
(315) 733-0040

Bed Breakfast Network of NY
Suite 602, 134 West 34th Street
New York, NY 10001
(212) 645-8134

Bed & Breakfast Rochester
P.O. Box 444
Fairport, NY 14450
(716) 223-8877 or 223-8510

Bed & Breakfast U.S.A., Ltd.
(New York City, NY state, western Massachusetts)
P.O. Box 606
Croton-on-Hudson, NY 10520
(914) 271-6228 (Monday to Friday, 10:00 A.M. to 4:00 P.M.)

Rainbow Hospitality
(Western New York, southern Ontario, Canada)
9348 Hennepin Avenue
Niagara Falls, NY 14304
(716) 754-8877 or 283-4794

NORTH CAROLINA

Bed & Biscuits
P.O. Box 19664
Raleigh, NC 27619
(919) 787-2109 (Monday to Friday, 9:00 A.M. to 5:00 P.M.)

OREGON

Bed & Breakfast Accommodations—Oregon Plus
(Oregon, Washington, California, Vancouver and Victoria, B.C.)
5733 S.W. Dickinson Street
Portland, OR 97219
(503) 245-0642

PENNSYLVANIA

Bed & Breakfast Philadelphia
(Greater Philadelphia)
P.O. Box 630
Chester Springs, PA 19425
(215) 827-9650

Bed & Breakfast of Southeast Pennsylvania
Box 278, R.D. 1
Barto, PA 19504
(215) 845-3526

The Bed and Breakfast Traveler
(Philadelphia, Center City, Mainline, and suburbs)
P.O. Box 21
Devon, PA 19333
(215) 687-3565

Guest Houses
(Philadelphia, Wilmington, Baltimore, and Annapolis)
RD 9
West Chester, PA 19380
(215) 692-4575 (noon to 4 P.M.)

Pittsburgh Bed & Breakfast
2190 Ben Franklin Drive
Pittsburgh, PA 15237
(412)367-8080

RHODE ISLAND

Bed & Breakfast of Rhode Island, Inc.
(Statewide)
P.O. Box 3291
Newport, RI 02840
(401) 849-1298

Castle Keep Bed & Breakfast
(Newport)
44 Everett Street
Newport, RI 02840
(401) 846-0362

SOUTH CAROLINA

Historic Charleston Bed & Breakfast
43 Legare Street
Charleston, SC 29401
(803) 722-6606

TENNESSEE

Bed & Breakfast of Memphis
P.O. Box 41621
Memphis, TN 38174
(901) 726-5920

Host Homes of Tennessee
(Statewide)
P.O. Box 110227
Nashville, TN 37222-0227
(615) 331-5244

TEXAS

Bed & Breakfast Society of Texas
(Statewide)
921 Heights Boulevard
Houston, TX 77008
(713) 868-4654

Bed & Breakfast Texas Style, Inc.
(Statewide)
4224 W. Red Bird Lane
Dallas, TX 75237
(214) 298-8586 or 298-5433

VERMONT

Canoe Vermont
(Combined inn stays and canoe trips on Vermont rivers)
P.O. Box 610, Mad River Green
Waitsfield, VT 05673
(802) 496-2409

Vermont Bed & Breakfast
P.O. Box 1
East Fairfield, VT 05448
(802) 827-3927

VIRGINIA

Bensonhouse of Richmond, Va.
P.O. Box 15131
Richmond, VA 23222
(804) 648-7560 or 321-6277

Blue Ridge Bed & Breakfast
(Virginia, West Virginia, Maryland, Pennsylvania)
Rocks & Rills
Route 2, Box 3895
Berryville, VA 22611
(703) 955-1246

Guesthouses Bed & Breakfast
(Charlottesville, Albemarle County, Luray)
P.O. Box 5737
Charlottesville, VA 22905
(804) 979-7264

WASHINGTON

Pacific Bed & Breakfast Agency
(Washington state and British Columbia)
701 N.W. 60th Street
Seattle, WA 98107
(206) 784-0539

WISCONSIN

Bed & Breakfast of Milwaukee, Inc.
P.O. Box 1822
Waukesha, WI 53187-1822
(414) 544-0060

CANADA

BRITISH COLUMBIA

All Seasons Bed & Breakfast Agency
(Victoria, B.C.)
Box 5511, Station B
Victoria, British Columbia
Canada V8R 6S4
(604) 595-BEDS or 595-2337

ONTARIO

Niagara Region Bed & Breakfast Service
(Niagara Falls, Niagara on the Lake, Welland, St. Catherine's,
Port Colborne, Fort Erie)
2631 Dorchester Road
Niagara Falls, Ontario
Canada, L2J 2Y9
(416) 358-8988

QUEBEC

Montreal Bed & Breakfast
(Province of Quebec, Montreal, Laurentian Mts.)
4912 Victoria
Montreal, Quebec
Canada H3W 2N1
(514) 738-9410

ENGLAND

Leander Travel Inc.
(England and the British Isles)
2715 Garland Lawn
Plymouth, MN 55447
(612) 473-2911

FRANCE

Chez Vous, at Home in France
(Nationwide)
220 Redwood Highway, Suite 129
Mill Valley, CA 94941
(415) 331-2535

GERMANY

AAR AngloAmerican Reisebüro GMBH
Bodelschwingh Strasse 13
4535 Wesleckappein/FRG
Federal Republic of Germany
011-05-4042570

NEW ZEALAND

New Zealand Travel Hosts
(Nationwide)
279 Williams Street
Kaiapoi, Christchurch, New Zealand
Phone: Kaiapoi 6340

Note: Membership in the association changes from year to year. A current directory of member reservation services can be obtained by sending $1.00 and a legal-size self-addressed envelope to Bed & Breakfast Reservation Services Worldwide, P.O. Box 14797, Dept. 174, Baton Rouge, LA 70898.

Index